PATSY CLINE

In Her Own Words

OTHER BOOKS BY THE AUTHORS

Memphis Elvis-Style

The Best of Elvis

Patsy Cline

In Her Own Words

Letters to a Friend

Mike Freeman
Cindy Hazen

SARTORIS LITERARY GROUP

ISBN: 979-8-9871205-6-9

Cover photo: Courtesy of Patsy Cline Enterprises, LLC with appreciation to The Patsy Cline Museum

Author photos: Mary Freeman

SARTORIS LITERARY GROUP
Metro-Jackson, Mississippi
Sartorisliterary-dot-com

PATSY CLINE
In Her Own Words

The first photo Patsy sent to Treva.

From Treva's personal scrapbook, courtesy of Bruce Steinbicker.

CONTENTS

A FEW WORDS FROM CHARLIE DICK,
Widower of Patsy Cline

Reading these letters brought back a lot of memories for me. I can remember a lot of the things that Patsy wrote about. Some of them I'd forgotten.

Some of the things that Patsy mentions in her letters never happened at all. She wasn't making things up. I don't want you to get the wrong impression of Patsy; she wasn't being dishonest. But sometimes the record company made promises to her and she got excited and wrote to Treva. Then the record company didn't keep its promises. I've tried to help Cindy and Mike identify what actually happened and what didn't so that we can set the record straight.

Patsy thought a lot of Treva. She knew how hard Treva worked for her and she enjoyed her friendship. I can remember when Treva and Bruce came to see us in Winchester. They stopped by a few times. When Treva was killed, Patsy was really upset.

A lot of years have passed since then. After I read the letters, I got to thinking about Bruce. One night I gave him a call and we talked for about two hours. We had a lot of catching up to do. We did a lot of reminiscing. I was happy that the letters were found and that they are being published because it will help fans have a better picture of who the real Patsy Cline was. For our daughter, Julie, our son, Randy, and our grandchildren, it's another way for them to get to know her a little better. For all of you that never got a chance to meet her, let me tell you, Patsy was really something.

i

ii

FOREWORD

BY MARGO PRICE

The first time I heard Patsy Cline's voice haunt the air, I was just a child. My elementary school music teacher was putting together a talent show and had picked the song "Walkin' After Midnight" as a one of the solos that year. I wanted to sing that song more than anything on the face of the earth. I didn't know much about singing or heartbreak back then, but hearing Patsy's voice come through the speakers of a small cassette player sent a chill up my spine. Her vibrato gave me goosebumps and made the hair on the back of my neck stand straight up. Until hearing her recordings, that was something I had never experienced from music. It was otherworldly and although the song was simple, her delivery made it spiritual. At the age of nine years old, I didn't exactly know *who* she was looking for or *where* she was walking to or what exactly she was doing walking around after midnight, but I knew I wanted to do it, too.

Born in 1932 during the Great Depression, Patsy (her birth name was Virginia Patterson Hensley) never learned to read music, but she taught herself how to play piano at the age of eight. She grew up singing gospel music in the church but she thought religion was "problematic." Patsy sounded like an angel when she sang, but cussed like a truck driver and told dirty jokes that made men blush. She lived on Kent Street, which was considered, "the wrong side of the tracks" and despite her having drive and talent, most of the folks in her town judged her and said "she wouldn't

Margo Price

amount to a hill of beans."

She sang in clubs, fire-halls, juke joints and gin mills, drive-ins, county fairs and dive bars. She sang her way from the annual minstrel show and on the roof of the refreshment stand at the Winchester Royal Drive-In all the way to the Grand Ole Opry. Patsy was the American dream in action. Her voice could be soft and tender one moment and aggressive and boisterous in the next, much like her attitude. But that swagger and complexity is what set her apart from the herd.

Patsy transformed what it meant to be a not only a female country star but a star in general. She was the first country artist to cross over from country to pop and be on both charts at once. In a time when women were expected to act and perform a certain way, she was breaking the mold. She helped prove that the country music genre was not purely macho and that it was okay to be a strong woman with a strong voice.

Patsy was ahead of her time in so many ways. Without her artistry and attitude, I wouldn't be the performer I am today. I owe so much to her, along with so many other artists, both women and men, who have been touched by her legacy. She was a feminist before feminism even had a name. Of course, we all know she had a curvy figure and wore red lipstick, which eventually became her signature but she also wore men's trousers, on stage no less, in a time when it was incredibly frowned upon. In those pants, she sauntered her way past the stereotypes and gatekeepers. She kept on walking past many forces of resistance winning over so many of them with her talent and charm, showing a male dominated business, that women were more than capable of leading a band. That they were also more than capable about singing about a myriad of subjects previously unavailable to them. Her performances proved that ladies could also sing about dark themes like drinking and divorce. She didn't just open doors for the women before her, she kicked them all the way down.

Through poverty, abuse, heartbreak and tragedy, Patsy rose time and time again, unwilling to let life get the best of her. She had the strength of a boxer, more nerve than a government mule and had more character and charisma than one lone person should. She chased her dreams with fervor until she finally caught up with them. Patsy was just thirty years old when everything came to an untimely end but she lived a life so big, she left a legacy and a blueprint for how to live your life.

*Margo Price is a Nashville-based singer-songwriter who, after thirteen years of waitressing, playing local clubs and low budget touring, became an overnight success with her album, **Midwest Farmer's Daughter.** A year later she released **All American Made**, which featured Willie Nelson on the song "Learning to Lose." Three more studio albums followed, including **That's How Rumors Get Started** and **Strays**. When not appearing solo with her band, she joins Chris Stapleton, Tim McGraw and Willie Nelson on their tours.*

PATSY CLINE
In Her Own Words

Patsy and Treva 's first meeting at the Hillbilly Homecoming.
From Treva's personal scrapbook, courtesy of Bruce Steinbicker.

PREFACE

The letters were found in a jewelry box, perhaps the very same box where a young girl named Treva Miller kept her most prized possessions. They were treasured items, reminders of love, friendship, and realized dreams. We can imagine her taking the letters out from time to time and rereading them, just as we can picture her excitement when each letter arrived from the postman all crisp and new.

Treva died when she was twenty-two years old. The box was put away and forgotten, just as Treva's friendship with a country music singer named Patsy Cline slipped from all but their families' memories.

Bruce Steinbicker, Treva's husband, remarried. He stayed close to Treva's mother and aunt and helped care for them in their old age. After they passed away, it was a relative, one of Treva's cousins, who found the box and claimed them as she was cleaning out the house. She placed a call to the Country Music Hall of Fame, who in turn called our good friend Stephen Shutts. With Stephen and John and Heather Mozart, we bought the entire collection of letters. We've later bought their half.

From the moment we first touched the letters and read Patsy's own words, we knew that this wasn't an ordinary collection of country music memorabilia. For us, owning the letters wasn't about turning a quick profit by reselling them to autograph collectors. We were touched by something much deeper than monetary goals: the conviction that the collection was meant to be shared. We felt strongly that one particular letter, the one written from the Winchester Hospital, should be returned to Patsy's family.

Patsy left us long before she might have written her own autobiography. Her letters allow her to speak for herself, to share with us her deepest dreams and desires as well as her joys and sorrows. She's just twenty-three when she pens her first letter to Treva, so we meet a naive young woman struggling for success. Through her letters we are privy to the breakup of her marriage to her first husband, Gerald Cline, and Patsy's declaration, "I don't think I'll ever marry again!" Shortly after, we meet Charlie Dick, who quickly becomes the love of Patsy's life. We share the birth of Patsy and Charlie's daughter, Julie. And through it all we are witness to Patsy's exhausting schedule of recording sessions and seemingly endless tours. We watch as Patsy matures from a young, relatively unknown singer to a more worldly entertainer, and we see that in many ways, Patsy doesn't really change at all. She remains a warmhearted country girl.

For all that has been written about Patsy's colorful personality, it seems to us that perhaps too much is sometimes made of her brassy nature. She probably learned early on that to succeed in a male dominated business she would have to speak up and be heard. She'd grab a beer, sit down with the boys, and start the first joke. Sure, she was full of life. She could rattle off the four-letter words with the best of them. But this was only one side of her. For all her unconventional behavior, she was also very traditional. This is the Patsy that we meet in these letters, not the bawdy woman that the gossips speak of, but the one who was deeply in love with her husband. Charlie and her children meant everything to her.

The Patsy Cline who befriended Treva Miller was not then the legend that we speak of today. She was an ordinary person with real emotions and everyday problems. Through her letters we learn of her loneliness, her financial worries, her excitement at her burgeoning career, and even the strains of stardom. As aware as we are now of Patsy's remarkable appeal, it is sometimes hard to imagine that her success was so hard won. These letters bring us to a period when Patsy's professional career was just beginning. We witness the birth of a superstar in the most private of ways.

Beyond offering a personal view of Patsy Cline, this collection of letters is about friendship. From the introductory first letter throughout the continuing correspondence, we see Patsy and Treva's friendship deepen. Treva becomes Patsy's first fan club president and she works hard to promote her. Patsy keeps her informed of her career happenings, but she confides in her, too, sharing things she never intended to be printed in a fan club newsletter.

Although Treva's letters to Patsy were lost years ago, Patsy's responding correspondence addresses the things and the people that were important in Treva's life. Treva's boyfriend, Bruce Steinbicker, was a country music disc jockey in Pennsylvania. They met through the Louvin Brothers Fan Club when Treva wrote to him and asked him to play their records. He visited and eventually moved to Telford; he moved, in fact, into Treva's well-chaperoned house, where she lived with her mother and aunt. Patsy, in many of the letters, included a few lines for Bruce.

None of the correspondence is more poignant than the letters surrounding Treva's wedding in June 1958. She and Bruce were married little more than two years when she was killed in a car accident. They had no children.

Treva's death was like a sad omen. Not only were Patsy and Treva linked in friendship, but they shared a tragic fate. In 1961 Patsy was in a disfiguring automobile accident. In 1963 a plane crash claimed her life.

If Patsy and Treva were alive today, they would be equally surprised at the interest in their story. Bruce has said that Treva couldn't possibly have imagined that anyone would be reading letters sent to her. That others would find those letters worth attention would have thrilled her. Patsy too would have been amazed. Nothing in Patsy's life would have led her to believe that she would become a star even bigger than her dreams.

Although Patsy recorded just three albums in her lifetime, she is one of country music's most recognized and beloved names. Her Greatest Hits compilation, released in 1967, is certified diamond by RIAA for ten million album sales. Three Grammy Awards were presented decades after her tragic death, and Patsy's music still finds fans with each new generation.

Until now, in our search to know Patsy Cline, we were left with the words of those who remember her. However, the letters found in Treva's jewelry box allow us to view Patsy's life from her own perspective. Music historians and even well-versed fans will discover discrepancies between Patsy's writings and what has been documented to now, especially with regard to recording session dates. We have tried to clarify, in text boxes, any inconsistencies and identify the events and people that Patsy talks about.

We've organized the letters by year and offer a short chapter at the start of each section to provide context and an overall view of events. In transcribing her letters, we have tried to stay true to Patsy's spelling or punctuation. After all, Patsy was a singer, not a writer.

The handwritten letters have a charm and an immediacy that is lost in typewritten copies. They bring us instantly to the fifties, where we can imagine Patsy sitting at the kitchen table and jotting a few lines before cooking supper or writing a few paragraphs while en route to the next show. As we personally immersed ourselves in the letters and the story that unfolded within their pages, we found a lot left to our imagination. It was many months later, almost two years after holding the first letter, that we visited Bruce Steinbicker, who pulled out Treva's scrapbook. It was like watching a movie after hearing the soundtrack, especially since Patsy, in her letters, often mentioned that she was including photographs. We're very pleased to include some of those photos in this book.

The pictures that Treva had so carefully placed on the oversized black pages of her scrapbook brought life to all the people we had been reading about. At last Treva had a face, young, happy, and obviously in love, much as we had imagined her but now viewed with an even greater sadness. Looking at the pictures of Patsy we're moved by her sheer joy. Although photographs are mute, so many seem bursting with laughter and song that it strikes us that Patsy was born to be in front of the camera as much as she was destined to stand before a microphone.

To us, that's really what the letters and what this book is about: life, love, music, and the power of dreams. They are all meant to be shared rather than hidden away in a box for safekeeping or framed on a private collector's wall.

ACKNOWLEDGEMENTS

We are indebted to Charlie Dick, Patsy's widower, for his cooperation. We want to thank Julie Fudge and Randy Dick for letting us share their mother's life. We can never repay Bruce Steinbicker for his kindness and generosity. Margo Price has our heartfelt appreciation for her contribution.

Stephen Shutts and John and Heather Mozart made the purchase of this collection of letters possible

Jimmy K. Walker of the Always Patsy Cline Fan Club helped us solve last-minute research problems.

Mark Medley, Kevin Fleming and the Country Music Hall of Fame have been a tremendous help.

Laura Kalpakian has freely offered advice, moral support, and inspiration.

We're grateful to Sue Freeman for her support and assistance with manuscript preparation.

Memphis Professional Imaging for their excellent work.

James L. Dickerson contributed valuable editorial assistance.

Last, but certainly not least, we want to thank Patsy and Treva.

Love and luck.

AUTHOR'S NOTE

Typewritten transcriptions of each of Patsy's letters follow the images of her handwritten letters. You may notice misspellings, odd punctuation or exaggerated words that she used for emphasis. We have tried to transcribe them exactly as they were written because they more fully reflect her personality.

PATSY CLINE
In Her Own Words

Patsy Cline performing in Nashville.
Photo courtesy the Nashville Tennessean.

1955

The road to stardom is seldom direct, especially for the impatient. In hindsight, success can seem quick and true, but this can never honestly be said of Patsy Cline's career. Hers was full of golden opportunities and critical acclaim with an equal measure of delays and false starts.

By the age of twenty-three Patsy Cline had been trying to push her career forward for more than seven hard years, singing on local radio and at supper clubs in her hometown of Winchester, Virginia, and the surrounding area. She'd quit high school to help support her mother and siblings, taking a full-time job at Gaunt's Drugstore while regularly performing late nights. She used every opportunity to promote herself to everyone she came across who was even remotely connected to the music business. Even her marriage in 1953 to Gerald Cline did not keep Patsy from singing. Her first husband wanted her to quit her budding career and stay home. She refused to give in. Gerald was destined to leave little in Patsy's life but his last name.

If fate had destined her a star early on, her appearance on Roy Acuff's "Dinner Bell" radio program on Nashville's WSM in 1948 surely would have transformed her, for all of the praise that it won her. The signing of a record contract with 4 Star Records in 1954 might have moved her along a little more quickly. Lesser artists might have been satisfied with those small accomplishments, but not Patsy Cline. She knew exactly what she wanted.

The year 1955 saw Patsy inching toward her goals. In retrospect this was a year of profound importance, and it seems that Patsy knew that this was a turning point." I can't believe this is happening to me," she said in her first letter to Treva Miller. Her enthusiasm and wonderment are so contagious that one feels perched on the brink of success with her, but the day-by-day accomplishments were less miraculous. The stardom that Patsy longed for did not come with any one particular event. It was instead the product of many seemingly small steps, and, while perhaps exciting at the time, their significance is only more apparent with today's perspective.

Certainly, the most important event of 1955 was Patsy's first recording session midyear in Nashville. The result, "A Church, A Courtroom, and Then Goodbye" backed with "Honky Tonk Merry Go Round," was met with little fanfare, largely because it was not promoted. While it did not immediately transform her into an overnight sensation, it introduced her to the man who would produce all but possibly one of her records, Owen Bradley.

The session was held at Bradley Film and Recording Studios, a business opened earlier that year by Owen and his brother, Harold, in a run-down neighborhood near downtown Nashville. It was the first recording studio to open in what is now known as Music Row. Owen was an accomplished musician and a talented arranger, and by 1955 he had gained considerable experience in the studio. While Patsy was relatively unknown and signed to a small label, the decision to place her with Bradley is an indication that there were larger forces at work, best understood by looking at Patsy's recording contract.

Patsy was signed with 4 Star Records, a label that had moderate success with the Maddox Brothers & Rose and T. Texas Tyler. It was their artist, Jimmy Dean, who most likely influenced Patsy's decision to join the 4 Star roster, if for no other reason than that at she knew him. Patsy had met Dean just weeks earlier in 1954 while appearing on the radio show

"Town and Country Time." His 4 Star record "Bummin' Around" was a Top Ten hit in 1953.

William McCall, 4 Star's owner, was a shrewd man who saw opportunity in Patsy. The fine points of the three-page legal document seemed like standard fare to the naive young woman. One clause in particular she would later regret: "The musical compositions to be recorded shall be mutually agreed upon between you and us, and each recording shall be subject to our approval." Unknowingly, Patsy signed away her rights to record any songs other than those that Bill McCall selected. With her artistic rights neatly tied up, McCall was assured of earning a larger share of the pie; in addition to his label royalties, he would get publishing royalties on everything Patsy recorded because he would only approve songs that he owned. In some instances, he shared writers' royalties too. Patsy would earn a meager 2.34 percent artist's royalty, half of the industry standard. The deal was accepted by Patsy and witnessed by Bill Peer, who was acting as her manager.

As headstrong as Patsy was, if McCall had convinced her of the benefits to her career, she most likely would have signed the contract regardless of what anyone else advised her. Likewise, she would have been the first to go against her manager's wishes if she detected a raw deal. The truth is, she and Bill Peer both thought this was a contract to be celebrated.

While Peer had Patsy's interests at heart, his industry experience was limited to the bookings he secured for his band, the Melody Boys. These were always weekend gigs so as not to conflict with the sales jobs he held during the week. Patsy had been a part of his group since 1952 and their relationship was rumored to be more intimate. By all accounts he would do anything to please her. What she wanted most was a recording career. Peer arranged for Patsy to make some demo tapes and he began shopping them. He went to work selling Patsy to Bill McCall with more fervor than the Buicks or washing machines he normally sold.

The record deal that Peer secured had its limitations, but it also had certain advantages. McCall basically ran a publishing house. Recording sessions were charged to the artists, and then the product was leased to the labels. As soon as he had Patsy on board, he set out to interest Decca in his new young artist. He arranged a trip to New York and studio time to record some demos. Paul Cohen, Decca's Artists and Repertoire (A&R) director for its country division, was in charge.

Cohen liked what he heard, so much so that he offered to buy Patsy's contract. McCall wouldn't sell. Then there was debate as to what songs Patsy would sing, but McCall was adamant that the only songs considered would be ones owned by 4 Star. Finally, Cohen signed the leasing and distribution contract, regrettably leaving McCall with more control than he would have liked.

One can't help but wonder what might have happened in Patsy's career if she had met Paul Cohen before William McCall. Would she have risen to the top more quickly as a full-fledged member of the Decca stable of artists? The argument could be made that Patsy's career was held back by the lackluster material that she was forced to record. Once the 4 Star contract expired in 1960 Patsy's records began to soar.

Perhaps it wouldn't have made any difference at all if Patsy had been under contract to Decca. As it was, the agreement reached in New York was that Patsy's records would be marketed by Decca as if they were Decca's own. The lack of promotional support the company provided for Patsy's first release might have been equivalent to that of any artist who had not yet demonstrated record sales.

What Decca did provide was expertise in the studio. It gave Paul Cohen the power to select the musicians and the arranger. He chose Owen Bradley, with whom he had worked for several years, to produce the session. McCall was the one who made the phone call to Bradley. "I'm going to send you a girl to record," Bradley remembered McCall saying. "She's mean as hell and hard to get along with." With that introduction, Bradley was prepared for the worst. He was pleasantly surprised to find Patsy cordial. She did everything asked of her.

This wasn't exactly a precedent for their relationship. They both were strong-willed. Bradley knew precisely the sound that he wanted from his artists and he could be very direct. Patsy had her own vision and didn't hesitate to say what she thought. They were sometimes at odds, but Patsy usually acquiesced. Bradley always got the sound that he was looking for.

Today he is often credited with contributing to Patsy's longevity because the quality that he was insistent upon achieving was ageless.

Patsy's voice has stood the test of time. The depth and emotion that she gave to a song will never go out of style. In the session held on June 1, 1955 at the Bradley Film and Recording Studios in Nashville, four songs were recorded: "A Church, A Courtroom and Then Goodbye," "Hidin' Out," "Turn The Cards Slowly," and "Honky Tonk Merry Go Round."

The lyrics to her first recording released on Decca's subsidiary label, Coral, "A Church, a Courtroom, and Then Goodbye," may seem a little maudlin by today's standards, but no one can argue the feeling that Patsy conveys. She sang as if baring the depths of her soul. In hindsight, one wonders if she was. Patsy's two-year marriage to Gerald Cline was coming to a close when this song was recorded.

Patsy was tidying up her personal life. Before the year would end, she would sever her relationship with Bill Peer. Despite his efforts to promote Patsy, he would never share in her success. Still, the record that he helped make a reality was important in another way. With this record, another important person came into Patsy's life, a seventeen-year-old girl named Treva Miller.

Treva was a small-town east Tennessee girl who shared Patsy's passion for country music. She might not have been as bold as Patsy, but she was not shy. Already she was active in several fan clubs and writing her own country music newsletter. We may never know if she happened to see one of Patsy's early shows or if she simply heard her on the radio, but wherever she was introduced to Patsy's music she fell in love with it. She decided to meet the woman behind the voice and wrote a letter

From Treva's personal scrapbook, courtesy of Bruce Steinbicker.

introducing herself. What's more, she had something to offer Patsy: She wanted to start a fan club for Patsy if the singer didn't have one already.

Treva became one of Patsy's greatest promoters, a champion at the grass roots level. She also became a good friend. And it all started with one letter written in the fall of 1955.

Winchester, Va.
Oct, 29/55

Dear Treva:

I will answer your most welcome letter which I received some time ago. It was soo nice of you to take an interest in me, so I'll try to let you know a little about my self.

"A Church, A Courtroom, Then Goodbye" was my first record, and by Now, the 7th I'll have another out called "Turn The Cards Slowly" Vs. "Hidin Out". On Now the 19th I'll appear on T.V. with Red Foley on the Ozark Jubilee, which I still cant believe is happening to me. Ever since I was four years old I've dreamed and prayed that some day I might be able to hear my self on record, and to be an entertainer. Now that I'm going to do just that, I still cant believe it.

It all started Treva, when I was 8 years old in Lexington Va, where I received a piano for my birthday. Then up through the years I began to play for church, and play & sing with my Mother at Home

II.

prayer meetings. At the age of sixteen, In Winchester I had to stop school to help Mother keep the home and my brother & sister in school. I worked every day and at nite sang for anything where I could be heard. In 1948, I went to Nashville, Tenn, for an audition. While there, I sang with Roy Acuff on his Dinner Bell Program over W.S.M. Was asked to stay in Nashville, but I had to return home with Mom & the children. I still didn't give up. Then I started singing with "Bill Peer & the Melody Boys" over W.E.P.M. Martinsburg, W.Va. & W.I.N.C. Winchester, Va. singing at dances & shows. Then in 1954 I signed with 4 Star Record Co. but didn't make any records until 1955 this past July. While in my recarding session it was decided that I could be put over on Carol Records, which I was really tickled about. So when my first record came out, it was on Carol. While in Nashville this past July, I appeared on the Grande Ole Opry with Ernest Tubb & also on T.V. with him.

He is the dearest & most wonderful man in the country music field I think. He

III

has surley been a helping hand for me, along with, Jimmy Dickens, Roy Acuff, Faron Young, Mr. Jack Stapp, Mr. Bill McCall, and Bill Peer, my band leader & manager. Of course, the ones who were always there when I needed them, my Mother and the Man up- stairs.

My Mother, Mrs. Hilda Hensley, makes all of my clothes, while I design them.

Inclosed you will find a small picture which I hope you can use. I am 23 years of age, stand 5 ft 5½ in, weight 135 lbs. and have brown hair & eyes. My favorite foods are chicken and spaghettie. Also collect, salt & pepper shakers, and earrings.

Treva, I hope some day to be able to thank you in person, and all the many friends like Bob Jennings & Ernest Tubb & others. I know that I would never have made it with out the help and kindness of friends and the man up stairs.

After my trip to the Ozarks I'll return home for Christmas with the family, and then in Jan. some time, back to Nash- ville, Tenn, and to the Grande Ole Opry.

III

has surley been a helping hand for me, along with, Jimmy Dickens, Roy Acuff, Faron Young, Mr. Jack Stapp, Mr. Bill McCall, and Bill Peer, my band leader & manager. Of course, the ones who were always there when I needed them, my Mother and the Man up-stairs.

My Mother, Mrs. Hilda Hensliy, makes all of my clothes, while I design them.

Inclosed you will find a small picture which I hope you can use. I am 23 years of age, stand 5 ft 5½ in, weight 135 lbs, and have brown hair & eyes. My favorite foods are chicken and spaghettie. Also collect, salt & pepper shakers, and earrings.

Treva, I hope some day to be able to thank you in person, and all the many friends like Bob Jennings & Ernest Tubb & others. I know that I would never have made it with out the help and kind ness of friends and the man up stairs.

After my trip to the Ozarks, I'll return home for Christmas with the familey, and then in Jan. some time, back to Nash-ville, Tenn, and to the Grande Ole Opry.

II.

Thanks again and hope to meet your friend Max Lowe, in the future. If he is in the Country music field, he's a friend of mine. Hopeing to hear from you soon.

Musically Yours,

Patsy Cline.

P.S.   As yet Treva, I don't have a fan club, and would you please send me the information on just what it does and what all there is to do to get one started?   Thank You.

PATSY CLINE

Winchester, Va.
Oct. 29/55

Dear Treva:

I will answer your most welcome letter which I received some time ago. It was so nice of you to take an interest in me, so I'll try to let you know a little about myself.

"A Church, A Courtroom, Then Goodbye," was my first record, and by Nov. the 7th I'll have another out called "Turn The Cards Slowly," b/w "Hidin Out ." On Nov the 19th I'll appear on T.V. with Red Foley on the Ozark Jubilee, which I still can't believe is happening to me. Ever since I was four years old, I've dreamed and prayed that someday I might be able to hear myself on a record, and to be an entertainer. Now that I'm going to do just that, I still can't believe it.

It all started Treva, when I was 8 years old in Lexington Va., where I received a piano for my birthday. Then up through the years I began to play for church, and play and sing with my Mother at Home prayer meetings. At the age of sixteen, in Winchester, I had to stop school to help Mother keep the home and my brother and sister in school. I worked every day and at night sang for anything where I could be heard. In 1948, I went to Nashville, Tenn., for an audition. While there, I sang with Roy Acuff on his Dinner Bell Program over W.S.M. Was asked to stay in Nashville, but I had to return home with Mom and the children. I still didn't give up. Then I started singing with "Bill Peer and The Melody Boys" over W.E.P.M. Martinsburg, W.Va. and W.I.N.C. Winchester, VA., singing at dances and shows. Then in 1954 I signed with 4 Star Record Co. but didn't make any records until 1955 this past July. While in my recording session it was decided that I could be put over on Coral Records, which I was really tickled about. So when my first record came out, it was on Coral. While in Nashville this past July, I appeared on the Grand Ole Opry with Ernest Tubb and also on T.V. with him. He is the dearest and most wonderful man in the country music field I think. He has surely been a helping hand for me, along with Jimmy Dickens, Roy Acuff, Faron Young, Mr. Jack Stapp, Mr. Bill McCall, and Bill Peer, my band leader and manager. Of course, the ones who were always there when I needed them, my Mother and the Man Upstairs. My Mother, Mrs. Hilda Hensley, makes all of my clothes, while I design them.

Enclosed you will find a small picture which I hope you can use. I am 23 years of age, stand 5 ft 5½ in, weight 135 lbs., and have brown hair and eyes. My favorite foods are chicken and spaghetti. Also collect salt and pepper shakers, and earrings.

Treva, I hope someday to be able to thank you in person, and all the many friends like Bob Jennings and Ernest Tubb and others. I know that I would never have made it without the help and kindness of friends and the Man Upstairs.

After my trip to the Ozarks, I'll return home for Christmas with the family, and then in Jan. some time, back to Nashville, Tenn, and to the Grand Ole Opry. Thanks again and I hope to meet your friend Max Lowe in the future. If he is in the Country Music field, he's a friend of mine. Hoping to hear from you soon.

Musically yours,
Patsy Cline

PS. As yet Treva, I don't have a Fan club, and would you please send me the information on just what it does and what all there is to do to get one started? Thank You.

Ernest Tubb, Jimmy Dickens, Roy Acuff, and Faron Young, were well-known entertainers. Jack Stapp was the program director at WSM, a popular Nashville radio station. He later founded Tree Publishing Company, one of the largest publishers of country music. Faron was inducted into the Country Music Hall of Fame in 2000.

•

The Saturday night Grand Ole Opry on WSM Nashville is the oldest continuous radio program. It is also the spiritual home of country music. Although the performance fee is minimal, appearing on the "Opry" is considered an honor. From October 1955 to September 1956 ABC television network broadcast one hour of the "Opry."

Winchester, Va
Nov 9, 55.
Wed. Nite.

Dear Treva;

Received your welcome letter and was glad to hear from you again. You make me feel like I've known you all my life, but that's how I like people.

You sound like you are a busy little girl, but if you like Country Music like I do, you enjoy every bit of it. I'm getting songs ready for another recording session in about two wks.

My bass man called me yesterday and tells me I may have to wait until the 26th. of Nov. instead of the 19th. to go to the Ozark Jubilee. So I'll have to drop you a card as to the exact date when he calls me, which I'll know in a couple of days.

I've answered your questions as best I could. I would say, the greatest song ever written was "Satisfied Mind", but of course it was "Just A Closer Walk With Thee" that put me where I am today. I sang it the first time I was in Nashville and sang it on the Dinner Bell Program with Roy Acuff, then I went to the Opry in July 55 I sang it, because Ernest Tubb thinks there

II

is no one who can sing it like I can. "God Bless Him". And it happened to be the song I sang when Walley Fowler first heard me sing in 1948. Thats when he set up an audition in Nashville for me.

About musical instruments, I use to play the piano (from age 8 to 16) but now I dont fool with it at all.

Of course, the biggest thrill was when I stepped out on the Grande Ole Opry stage.

Yes I'm married to a wonderfull guy from Frederick, Md. where I've lived for 2 years½. But now we live with Mom until we can get a trailer. We've been married for 3 years.

We don't have any children as yet. We lost one, but hope to have some one day.

Thanks for the pictures you sent me, and tell May "hello" for me & "good luck."

Thanks also for the Fan Club information. I'm waiting a little while until people know who Patsy Cline is a little better and then I'll start a Club.

Well, I guess I'd better close & get supper ready. You write soon and let me know how things are. It's snowing here tonite - Our first. So long for now

Love & Luck,
Patsy Cline.

Questions

Q. When and where were you born?

A. In Winchester, Va. Sept 8th 1932

Q. How long have you been singing?

A. 16 years. but Professionally 9 years.

Q. Who gave you your first break?

A. Wally Fowler ~~made~~ it possible for me to sing at W.S.M.

Q. What Musical instruments do you play?

A. Piano.

Q. What is your all time favorite song?

A. Satisfied Mind. or Just A Closer Walk With Thee.

Q. What was the biggest thrill to you in your career?

A. When I sang on the Grande Ole Opry. In July 1955

Q. Are you Married?

A. Yes. Have been for 3 years.

Winchester, Va
Nov. 9/55
Wed. Nite.

Dear Treva:

Received your welcome letter and was glad to hear from you again. You make me feel like I've known you all my life, but that's how I like people.

You sound like you are a busy little girl, but if you like Country Music like I do, you enjoy every bit of it. I'm getting songs ready for another recording session in about two weeks.

My boss man called me yesterday and tells me I may have to wait until the 26th. of Nov. instead of the 19th to go to the Ozark Jubilee. So I'll have to drop you a card as to the exact date when he calls me, which I'll know in a couple of days.

I've answered your questions as best I could. I would say, the greatest song ever written was "Satisfied Mind," but of course it was "Just A Closer Walk With Thee" that put me where I am today. I sang it the first time I was in Nashville and sang it on the Dinner Bell Program with Roy Acuff. Then I went to the Opry in July 55. I sang it, because Ernest Tubb thinks there is no one who can sing it like I can. (God Bless Him). And it happened to be the song I sang when Walley Fowler first heard me sing in 1948. That's when he set up an audition in Nashville for me.

About musical instruments, I used to play the piano (from age 8 to 16) but now I don't fool with it at all.

Of course, the biggest thrill, was when I stepped out on the Grand Ole Opry stage.

Yes I'm married to a wonderful guy from Frederick, Md. where I've lived for 2 years. But now we live with Mom until we can get a trailer. We've been married for 3 years. We don't have any children as yet. We lost one, but hope to have some one day.

Thanks for the pictures you sent me, and tell Max "hello" for me and "good luck."

Thanks also for the Fan Club information.

I'm waiting a little while until people know who Patsy Cline is a little better and then I'll start a Club.

Well, I guess I'd better close and get supper ready. You write soon and let me know how things are. It's snowing here tonight. Our first. So long for now.

Love and luck,
Patsy Cline

Questions:

Q. When and where were you born?
A. In Winchester, Va. Sept 8th 1932

Q. How long have you been singing?
A. 16 years, but professionally 9 years.

Q. Who gave you your first break?
A. Wally Fowler made it possible for me to sing at W.S.M.

Q. What musical instruments do you play?
A. Piano.

Q. What is your all-time favorite song?
A. Satisfied Mind or Just A Closer Walk With Thee

Q. What was the biggest thrill for you in your career?
A. When I sang on the Grand Ole Opry. In July 1955

Q. Are you married?
A. Yes. Have been for 3 years.

Wally Fowler was best known for promoting gospel music shows at the Ryman Auditorium which were broadcast over WSM. When he performed in Winchester in 1948, teenage Patsy wrangled an audition. He invited her to sing on his show that night

•

The Ozark Jubilee in Springfield, Missouri, was hosted by country music singer Red Foley and, on ABC was the most successful country music television show of the 1950s.

•

Patsy never learned to read music. She played and sang by ear.

Winchester, Va
Dec. 26, /55

Dear Treva:

Well it sure was nice to hear from you, and I'm sorry I haven't written to you sooner, but I've just got back from a recording session in Nashville, which was on Dec. 18th, and I also appeared in the Opry, and on January 7th I'm going to be on T.V coast to coast with the Opry — so tune me in gal. I'm soo happy about it I could pop. Ha! I don't know if I told you about it or not, but I'm appearing on T.V.

you, I hope.

Also I want to congratulate you on such a fine book and also the 2nd issue your just out (?) of your journal. I really enjoy reading about all the different subject of the country music world, and finding out what, where, & who?

You sure did a fine job on Martha's story but I guess Oh! By the way, Irma, Jimmy Dean (He now has a recording out on Mercury) & Buck Ryan, who walks with Jimmy's band, would you like to tell you I represent them. You could write them at the address here. (Pretty

merry Sat. nite in Washington with "Town & Country Time" with Jimmy Dean, & the Texas Wild Cats. W.M.A.L. Chanl 7. Wash. D.C. and I came (?) when I have some place to go, they always let me off. And Mr. Brizell ways let me off. And Mr. Brizell says his appear to 32 on tour days after this trip to Nashville again for the T.V. show. I'll be singing one of my new song I just recorded. Enough of me. Now I want you to know I really think you far the things you are doing for me, Irma. I just wish I could thank you enough. Maybe someday I'll be able to do same thing to help you.

W.M.A.L. Television Station.
Conn. Ave. N.W.
Washington, D.C.
I certainly do wish you the
best of luck in starting your
Jamboree, you & Bruce.
Talking about me doing some
hymns. Yes! I'm going to record
some hymns next session.
Oh! By the way. Treva, I'm not
with Bill Peer any more & he's not
my personal manager, any more.
Well, I guess I'm out of gossip
so you write soon & I hope to be
looking at you on Jan. 7th. 56.
Tell Mae, Bruce, & all the D.J.
at W.F.H.C. in Bristol hello for me
& a Happy New Year to all. Always
Patsy Cline

Winchester, Va.
Dec. 26/55

Dear Treva:

Well it sure was nice to hear from you, and I'm sorry I haven't written
to you sooner, but I've just got back from a recording session in Nashville,
which was on Dec. 18th, I also appeared on the Opry, and on January 7th
I'm going to be on T.V. coast to coast with the Opry, so tune me in.

I'm soo happy about it I could pop. Ha. I don't know if I told you about
it or not, but I'm appearing on T.V. every nite in Washington with "Town
and Country Time" with Jimmy Dean, and The Texas Wild Cats. W.M.A.L.
Channel 7. Wash. D.C. and of course when I have some place to go, they
always let me off. And Mr. McCall says I'm suppose to go on tour after
this trip to Nashville again for the T.V. show. I'll be singing one of my new
songs I just recorded. Enough of me.

Now I want you to know I really thank you for the things you are
doing for me Treva. I just wish I could thank you enough. Maybe someday
I'll be able to do something to help you, I hope.

Also I want to congratulate you on such a fine book and also the 2nd
issue you put out of your Journal. I really enjoy reading about all the
different subjects of the country music world, and finding out what, where,
and who.

You sure did a fine job on Martha's story and mine too.

Oh! By the way, Treva, Jimmy Dean (who now has 4 recordings out
on Mercury) and "Buck Ryan" who works with Jimmy's band, would like
to have you to represent them. You could write them at the address here.

Jimmy Dean
WM.A.L. Television Station
Conn. Ave. N.W.
Washington, D.C.

I certainly do wish you the best of luck in starting your jamboree, you
and Bruce.

Talking about me doing some hymns. Yes! I'm going to record some hymns next session.

Oh! By the way. Treva, I'm not with Bill Peer any more and he's not my personal manager, any more.

Well, I guess I'm out of gossip so you write soon and I hope to be looking at you on Jan. 7th 56.

Tell Max, Bruce, and all the DJ.'s at W.F.H.A. in Bristol hello for me and a Happy New Year to all. Always.

Patsy Cline

'Town and Country Time' was a popular show in the D.C. area. Jimmy Dean was its star performer. In 1957 he hosted his own show on CBS with many of the same cast members. He continued to sing and host television shows and is best known today for his sausage company.

•

This is the first mention of Bruce Steinbicker, who will later marry Treva.

•

The December 18 session that Patsy mentions is not listed in any discography. It's likely the session was postponed until January 5, 1956.

**Patsy in the studio with Paul Cohen, A&R director for
Decca's country music division**
From Treva's personal scrapbook, courtesy of Bruce Steinbicker.

1956

Nineteen fifty-six was Elvis Presley's year. Starting with a regional following and a new contract with RCA, he went on, in a twelve-month period, to earn a few gold records, appear on the country's top television shows, grace the cover of a whole lot of magazines, and film his first movie. His success was phenomenal, and it was not lost on Patsy. When Decca told her it was going to push her song "Walkin' After Midnight" the way Presley was pushed, she excitedly wrote to Treva. Her dreams were every bit as big as Elvis's. They were just slower to be realized.

Judging from Patsy's letters, her life and career in 1956 was a series of postponements. The one constant was the support of Connie B. Gay. He had built a small country music empire in the Washington, D.C., area with his "Town and Country Time" and "Town and Country Jamboree" television shows and traveling package tours. Patsy was a regular and she was becoming something of a celebrity in the shows' viewing area.

Nowhere is this more evident than her appearance at Winchester's Apple Blossom Festival in April. Being honored in her hometown was a thrill for Patsy, first experienced the previous year when she appeared with Bill Peer and the Melody Boys. This year she was a solo act. A banner on the side of the automobile proclaimed *Town & Country T.V. Star-Patsy Cline*. Her sister, Sylvia, sat next to her, but there was no mistaking the star. With a white hat perched on her head, a white scarf tied smartly around her neck, and a full-fringed costume, she looked as though she had just stepped off the television screen. A month earlier Patsy had been the cover story of the *Washington Star* Sunday magazine. She wore a similar outfit for that photo shoot.

This was the height of Patsy's cowgirl phase. She had worn western clothing for a few years, but as her audience increased so did her wardrobe. Patsy designed the dresses and her mother sewed them. The costumes became more and more elaborate with fringe, studs, appliques, and embroidery. Patsy was proud of them and often described them to Treva. She was creating an image that she hoped would carry her popularity outside the Washington/Virginia area.

Often the opportunity to reach a larger country music audience did not happen as she wished. Like so many of Patsy's plans her appearance on the *Ozark Jubilee* was delayed for several months. When at last she finally did appear, there was a mix-up in communication and instead of the two songs that she had selected she could only sing one.

Patsy also looked forward. to appearing on another big country music television show, California's "Town Hall Party." Unfortunately, that didn't materialize in 1956, nor did her dream of appearing on Arthur Godfrey's "Talent Scouts," though she tried out for the show in September.

Her lack of success wasn't due to lack of enthusiasm. The letters Patsy wrote to Treva are brimming with plans, no doubt because the people around her were enthusiastic. Some of these events happened as Patsy said they would, especially those relating to Connie Gay's "Town and Country" shows. But many more of these events never materialized. A prime example was a tour of Asia. In her letter to Treva dated March 19, Patsy wrote that she would be leaving May 6 to go to Japan and Korea for ninety days. She never mentioned the tour again.

We may never know why this particular deal fell through, but we can speculate. On April 13 Patsy met a fellow who turned her life upside down: Charlie Dick. By May 28 she was declaring that Charlie was buying her a diamond soon, and all this from a woman who just a few months earlier had vowed that she'd never marry again. Patsy's personal life was changing quickly. She'd started the year living with her husband Gerald. In February they moved into a brand-new mobile home. By March she was living at home with her mother in Winchester and planning a divorce.

Love might have kept her from traveling across the ocean, but it couldn't keep her at home. She was doing a lot of live shows, perhaps too many, given the tone of the letters. By August, Patsy complains that she hasn't had a Sunday off in three months. She's working every day and is still not making much money. She's tired of people, she says. Patsy is already feeling the strains of stardom, though she's not quite the star that she wants to be just yet.

The demands on her time might have been wearing, but Patsy never really tires of people. She's been in the business long enough that some of the younger artists look up to her. Patsy enjoys her role as mentor. As her confidence in Treva grows, she often asks for Treva's help in promoting these young singers.

Treva has been tirelessly promoting Patsy. The fan club was officially launched early in the year, complete with membership cards. Patsy keeps Treva informed of her comings and goings and all of her career news, and Treva takes note. By September Treva has put together a newsletter. Patsy is thrilled. "I didn't realize there was enough news on me to make a book," she says.

But there has been a lot of news throughout the year. By this time Patsy's career is starting to make headway. She was voted among the top ten female country singers in polls in Jamboree and Country Song Roundup magazines. She attended her first disc jockey convention in Nashville and schmoozed with the artists, disc jockeys, and record company executives.

By this time, she had released two records: "I Love You, Honey/ Come On In" on the Coral label and "I've Loved and Lost Again/ Stop Look and Listen" on the Decca label. Although these songs didn't chart, the record company was paying more attention to her. The move of Patsy's music to the Decca label from the Coral label was clearly a measure of faith.

"Walkin' After Midnight," Patsy's second record on the Decca label, was recorded in November, though not released this year. The flip side was a song that Patsy actually preferred, " A Poor Man 's Roses," perhaps because it spoke more personally to her. "I must make up my mind today, what to have and to hold," she sings. This song is more of a ballad, which is more to Patsy's taste. She's not yet comfortable with singing pop, though it's clear that her management recognizes her talent in this area. Reportedly Bill McCall persuaded Patsy to sing "Walkin' After Midnight," a fact that is astounding given that it was not a song that he owned. It was a song he believed in so much that he made an exception to the publisher's clause in her contract.

This was perhaps the single most significant decision of 1956. As the year ended a hit recording was in the works. Like Elvis, Patsy started the year with a regional audience. By the year's end she was ready to hit the national stage. Her career was gaining momentum.

Winchester, Va.
1/16/56

Dear Treva:

Just got a few min-
utes, so I'll drop you a
few lines.

I hope this finds you
well and things going
good for you.

As for me, I can't com-
plain. Things are going
pretty good for me. Last
Sunday I got back from
Nashville at 4. P.m after my
first plane trip, and it
was just grand. I wasn't
afraid at all after leaving
the ground.

While in Nashville I
stayed at the Andrew Jackson

54

II

Hotel & had the thrill of meeting T. Tommy and Bob Jennings and Jack Beasly. who are 3 wonderfull fellows. After the Opry last Sat. nite I went out to the Plantation Club, with Tony Bennett, Ray Price, Audrey Williams, Bill Morgan & Eddie Arnold, lots of publishers & writers. We had a party and a wonderfull time. They men called Tony, Eddie, Ray, Bill & I up to sing at the Plantation Club. I sang 2 songs & they would'nt let me set down so I sang another one. They were just wonderfull to me.

On the 11 of Feb. I'll be on the Ozark Jubilee for sure

III.

this time. There out to the "Town Hall" in California & then to the "Big D Jamboree" in Dallas Texas. & they said I could come back to the Opry by then - Of course in the between times, I'll be here in Washington on "Town & Country Time".

Well, I guess you are busy, and I must close & stop chin-chomping & get to bed.

Write real soon Treva & tell Max hello & tell him to keep up the good work.

By for now.

I'll write more next time. Love & good wishes

From Treva's personal scrapbook, courtesy of Bruce Steinbicker.

Winchester, Va.
1/16/56

Dear Treva:

    Just got a few minutes, so I'll drop you a few lines.

    I hope this finds you well and things going good for you.

    As for me, I can't complain. Things are going pretty good for me. Last Sunday I got back from Nashville at 4:PM after my first plane trip, and it was just grand. I wasn't afraid at all after leaving the ground.

    While in Nashville, I stayed at the Andrew Jackson Hotel and had the thrill of meeting T. Tommy, and Bob Jennings and Jack Beasley, who are 3 wonderful fellows.

    After the Opry last Sat. nite I went out to the Plantation Club, with Tony Bennett, Ray Price, Audrey Williams, Bill Morgan and Eddy Arnold, lots of publishers, and writers. We had a party and a wonderful time. They even called Tony, Eddy, Ray, Bill and I up to sing at the Plantation Club. I sang 2 songs and they wouldn't let me sit down so I sang another one. They were just wonderful to me.

    On the 11 of Feb. I'll be on the Ozark Jubilee for sure this time. Then out to the "Town Hall" in California and then to the "Big D Jamboree" in Dallas Texas, and they said I could come back to the "Opry" by then. Of course in the between times, I'll be here in Washington on "Town and Country Time."

    Well, I guess you are busy, and I must close and stop chinchomping and get to bed.

    Write real soon Treva and tell Max hello and tell him to keep up the good work.

Bye for now.

I'll write more next time. Love and good wishes.

Bob Jennings worked for WLAC radio in Nashville, and T. Tommy Cutrer for WSM. Jack Beasley worked in the recording industry in Nashville.

•

Ray Price and Eddy Arnold are members of the Country Music Hall of Fame. Audrey Williams was prominent because of her marriage to Hank Williams.

Hilda Hensley, Patsy's mother, sewed many of the costumes Patsy wore on stage.

From Treva's personal scrapbook, top & bottom, courtesy of Bruce Steinbicker.

A few of Patsy's costumes laid out on the couch in her home.

Winchester, Va
1/25/56.

Dear Irena:

Haven't heard from you but I had to get in touch with you right away Gal.

I've got to get a club president right away, because every one keeps asking me can they join my fan club, and I don't have any fan club except what you have been doing. A girl up here promised to be the ~~new~~ club president for me but she knew about as much as I do about it, and that's nothing. So I want you to take the job

II.

~~offcialty~~ ficially for me
and if you caift can you
sugest any one close up
here to me?

Let me know rite away
what you dicide by special
delivered and what I have to
do if any?

I havent got on around to
talk to Jimmy Dean but I
did foudnd out he does have
a fan club, by his mail.

I think the slips you
gave me are the slips I'd give
people if they wanted to join
my fan club for them to join
arent they?

I hope you know what
I mean? I dont know hardley
where I'm at today.

III.

I have had a cold and this past Saturday nite, and I didn't get to sing but 2 songs, and after that I couldn't even talk after the 2nd song. I'm glad it happened now instead of around the 11th of Feb when I'm going to the Ozark Jubilee. and Treva I got a letter yesterday from Nashville, saying in ~~April~~ April I'm to be back on the Opry on T.V. I'll let you know the date later on, and maybe you can come down & meet me there in Nashville and we could meet & have our pictures taken together to be put out for publicity.

Write me right away Treva. How have you ~~been~~ & Max? Tell him Hello & best of luck.

IV.

Well, I must close & get in touch with the director of the "Apple Blossom Parade" up here. I'm going to ride in it with a 56. Cadillac convertable eldarado to ride in.

The Washington Star Paper is coming out in about 4 weeks with a story and pictures of me.

I'm to be the Cover Girl on the magazine in color 18x20 with story in side. I'll send you a copy of it when it comes out.

Well let me hear from you real soon now because I'm got to get busy on it.

Hope you are well.

So long for now.

Love

Patsy C.

Winchester, Va.
1/25/56

Dear Treva:

Haven't heard from you but I had to get in touch with you right away
Gal.

I've got to get a club president right away, because everyone keeps
asking me can they join my fan club, and I don't have any fan club except
what you have been doing. A girl up here promised to be the club president
for me but she knew about as much as I do about it, and that's nothing. So
I want you to take the job officially for me and if you can't can you suggest
any one close up here to me?

Let me know rite away what you decide by special deliverer and what
I have to do if any?

I haven't got on around to talk to Jimmy Dean but I did find out he
does have a fan club, by his mail.

I think the slips you gave me are the slips I'd give people if they
wanted to join my fan club for them to join, aren't they?

I hope you know what I mean? I don't know hardly where I'm at today.
I have had a cold and this past Saturday nite, I didn't get to sing but 2
songs, and after that I couldn't even talk after the 2nd song. I'm glad it
happened now instead of around the 11th of Feb when I'm going to the
Ozark Jubilee, and Treva I got a letter yesterday from Nashville, saying in
April I'm to be back on the Opry on T.V. I'll let you know the date later on,
and maybe you can come down and meet me there in Nashville and we
could meet and have our pictures taken together to be put out for publicity.

Write me right away Treva. How have you been and Max? Tell him
hello and best of luck. Well, I must close and get in touch with the director
of the "Apple Blossom Parade" up here. I'm going to ride in it with a 56
Cadillac convertible Eldorado to ride in.

The Washington Star paper is coming out in about 4 weeks with a
story and pictures of me.

I'm to be the Cover Girl on the magazine in color, 18x20 with story *inside. I'll send you a copy of it when it comes out.*

Well let me hear from you real soon now because I've got to get busy on it.

Hope you are well. So long for now.

Love,

Patsy C.

Patsy and Treva did not meet in 1956.

•

Treva was well prepared to solve Patsy's dilemma over fan club operations. She had frequently corresponded with others involved in country music promotion.

Patsy Cline
Coral Recording Artist
Winchester, Virginia

Frederick, Md.
Feb 22/56

Dear Treva;

I guess you think I'm never going to answer your letter, but there are two reasons why I haven't writen sooner. I was moving to Frederick and the other, I just didn't have the money to send you yet. I still don't have it until next Thursday the 30th or 31st or what ever it is. I just moved in a 56, -33ft trailor, but I still can't say I'm satis-

II.

fied. Don't mention this in your
letters, but you know already (I
think told you.) I've been married 3½ years and in 55 in June
I left him because he's just soo
jealous of my ~~can't~~ singing, and
I was syperated six months. This
past Nov. we went back together
but I'm afraid things aren't
going to work out. He's 33. &
I'm 23. which I don't think has
anything to do with it but he
has been married befor. I'm his
3rd wife, and he dosent want
any children. Now he's starting
about my singing again. So

II.

Patsy Cline
Coral Recording Artist
Winchester, Virginia

I'm afraid things are not going
to be the same as they are now
in the next 6 months. I've tried
3 times and still I can't seem to
get what ever it is straightened
out. If things do come to a
point as a divorce I'm certainly not going to marry again.
Oh! well, I'm just telling you
my troubles so I'll stop for
now.
How are things with you?
They cancelled my Ozark appear-
ence again, But the Opry
called me the other day and

they want me back for 2 T.V.
shows iether in June, April, or
Aug. I'll let you know the date
when I get it.

The Apple Blossom Fet which
is in my home town, Winchester,
is going to have me in the
grand feature parade as the
T.V. personality (the only one) of the
Shenadoah Valley, sort of a lady
grande marshall, I guess you
would call it. Next Thurs. I'm
starting at Quantico for the
Marines. A 3 hour show there.
Just for the base & the fellows
I use to play there with The
Melody boys and they ask for

V

Patsy Cline
Coral Recording Artist
Winchester, Virginia

me back to sing for them. So
I guess I'm going back, and
they sure are a fine bunch of
fellows. Maybe we can get them
to join my fan club. Some of
them any way. About the picture
I'll send you a copy about
next week for the picture fan
club card for the fans. In
the mean time you can maybe
use this little one for something
The one I'm sending later will
be in my new costume. I'm
working on a new one with

V.

white horse s in rhinstones on it, in deep purple, with white fringe. Maybe I told you about it already. I'm soo mixed up lately.

Well, I'm going to close and get busy ironing, so write soon Treva and thanks for wait ing soo long for me, I'll sure send you the money as soon as I get it.

How is Max and how is he doing? Tell him hello for me.

And I'll write again soon.

You write to. If you can give me a little advance, write to 608. S, Kent St. Winchester. Love, Pat.

Frederick, Md.
Feb. 22/56

Dear Treva:

I guess you think I'm never going to answer your letter, but there are two reasons why I haven't written sooner.

I was moving to Frederick, and the other, I just didn't have the money to send you yet. I still don't have it until next Thursday the 30th or 31st or whatever it is. I just moved in a 56, 33ft trailer, but I still can't say I'm satisfied. Don't mention this in your letters, but you know already (I think I told you) I've been married 3½ years and in 55 in June I left him because he's just soo jealous of my singing, and I was separated six months. This past Nov. we went back together but I'm afraid things aren't going to work out. He's 33, and I'm 23, which I don't think has anything to do with it but he has been married before. I'm his 3rd wife, and he doesn't want any children. Now he's starting about my singing again. So I'm afraid things are not going to be the same as they are now in the next 6 months. I've tried 3 times and still can't seem to get whatever it is straightened out. If things do come to a point as a divorce I'm certainly not going to marry again.

Oh! Well, I'm just telling you my troubles so I'll stop for now.

How are things with you?

They cancelled my Ozark appearance again. But the Opry called me the other day and they want me back for 2 T.V. shows either in June, April, or Aug. I'll let you know the date when I get it.

The Apple Blossom Fet which is in my home town, Winchester, is going to have me in the grand feature parade as the T.V. personality (the only one,) of the Shenandoah Valley, sort of a lady grand marshal, I guess you would call it. Next Thurs. I'm starting at Quantico for the Marines. A 3 hour show there. Just for the base and the fellows. I use to play there with The Melody Boys and they ask for me back to sing for them. So I guess I'm going back, and they are a fine bunch of fellows. Maybe we can get them to join my Fan club. Some of them anyway. About the picture I'll send

73

you a copy about next week for the picture fan club card for the fans. In the mean time you can maybe use this little one for something.

The one I'm sending later will be in my new costume. I'm working on a new one with white horses in rhinestones on it, in deep purple, with white fringe. Maybe I told you about it already. I'm so mixed up lately.

Well, I'm going to close and get busy ironing, so write soon Treva and thanks for waiting so long for me, I'll sure send you the money as soon as I get it.

How is Max and how is he doing? Tell him hello for me. And I'll write again soon. You write too. If you can give me a little advance, write to 608. S. Kent St. Winchester.

Love, Pat.

Patsy married Gerald Cline on March 7, 1953. The son of a wealthy building contractor, he worked in the family business.

•

Patsy wore the purple and white fringed costume often.

Winchester, Va
March, 19/58

Dear Treva:

I haven't heard from you in a while, so I thought I'd drop you a line. I guess I haven't ~~heard~~ told you that I'm back home in Winchester, with Mom. So when you write; send it to 608 S. Kent.

He told me if I was gonna sing, I wasn't going to live with him. So I'm back home.

I'm sending you a copy of the Star paper and the story they put in the paper. You might be able to use it to some advantage.

They sure did a nice write up on me. And last Sat. night they had "Patsy Cline" night on T.V. in Washington for me. I signed my name I bet more

than I ever ~~had~~ ^happy in my life.
They people were wonderful to
me.

How is the fan club biz,
coming? Did you get my letters
that I sent you the money in?

I'd like to have a copy of the
club cards with the picture on the
end of it.

The April 7th has been set for
me on the Ozark Jubilee. And
on May 6th I'm to go over sea to
Japan & Korea with "Ann Jones
and her all girl band. for 90
days. I'm going with them I
think.

Well, I just wondered how you
were & how things were going?

You write soon & tell me all
the news. Tell Max hello & write
soon. Your Friend Always
Patsy Cline

Winchester, Va.
March 19/56

Dear Treva:

I haven't heard from you in a while, so I thought I'd drop a line. I guess I haven't told you that I'm back home in Winchester, with Mom. So when you write, send it to 608. S. Kent.

He told me if I was gonna sing, I wasn't going to live with him. So I'm back home.

I'm sending you a copy of the Star paper and the story they put in the paper. You might be able to use it to some advantage.

They sure did a nice write up on me. And last Sat. night they had "Patsy Cline" night on T.V. in Washington for me. I signed my name I bet more than I ever have in my life. The people were wonderful to me.

How is the fan club bis coming? Did you get my letter that I sent you the money in? I'd like to have a copy of the club cards with the picture on the end of it.

The April 7th has been set for me on the Ozark Jubilee. And on May 6th I'm to go over sea to Japan and Korea with Ann Jones and her all girl band, for 90 days. I'm going with them I think.

Well, I just wondered how you were and how things were going?

You write soon and tell me all the news. Tell Max hello and write soon.

Your Friend Always,
Patsy Cline

The trip to Asia never materialized. Patsy never traveled outside the United States.

•

Ann Jones and Her All Female Band were part of the "Town and Country" cast.

Patsy with her new 1956 Oldsmobile.
From Treva's personal scrapbook, courtesy of Bruce Steinbicker

Patsy Cline
Coral Recording Artist
Winchester, Virginia

April 10/56

Dear Treva:

Got your letters and was glad to hear from you again.

The pictures are fine and I've signed them all like you wanted

Was glad to hear from you and I'm sorry I haven't wrote to you befor this. I've been trying to get a new suit ready for the Apple Blossom Festival here on the 26th & 27th, and get ready for the 21st on the Jubilee. I'm also doing a session on the way back. Four new tunes, called, "I've Loved And Losted again", "Stop, Look, & Listen", with 2 secared songs too

#.

called "Dear God" and "He Will Do For You, What He's Done For Me". The Curr singers will help me on the Hymns.

I'm glad Bruce is coming to see you and I hope you have a good time during his stay. He writes to me once in a while to let me know how my records are doing up in Pa. He is very nice.

Well I got my self a car today, a 51 Hudson and I'm real proud of it. Got it all by my self. At least it will take me and bring me now.

Well the news here isn't to much, so I'll close for now and write more later. You are doing a wonderful job for Treva. I thank you. Loves Patsy.

April 10/56

Dear Treva:

Got your letters and was glad to hear from you again.

The pictures are fine and I've signed them all like you wanted.

Was glad to hear from you and I'm sorry I haven't wrote to you before this. I've been trying to get a new suit ready for the Apple Blossom Festival here on the 26th and 27th, and get ready for the 21st on the Jubilee. I'm also doing a session on the way back. Four new tunes, called, "I've Loved And Lost Again," "Stop, Look, and Listen," with 2 sacred songs too called, "Dear God" and "He Will Do For You, What He's Done For Me." The Kerr Singers will help me on the Hymns.

I'm glad Bruce is coming to see you and I hope you have a good time during his stay. He writes to me once in a while to let me know how my records are doing up in Pa. He is very nice.

Well I got myself a car today a 51 Hudson and I'm real proud of it. Got it all by myself. At least it will take me and bring me now.

Well the news here isn't too much, so I'll close for now and write more later. You are doing a wonderful job Treva. I thank you.

Love, Patsy

Patsy is referring to the Anita Kerr Singers. It would be a year before they would join her in the studio. The Anita Kerr Singers would record background vocals for many artists on Decca and RCA until 1963, when Anita withdrew from recording.

•

This was probably Bruce's first visit to Tennessee to see Treva.

Patsy Cline
Coral Recording Artist
Winchester, Virginia

April 18/56

Dear Irena:

Just a line to say hello and hope this finds you in the pink.

As far me I'm fine and as happy as if I had good sence. Ha.

This Sat. night I'll be on the Jubilee. I'm leaving Fri. morning at 8: A.m. and after the shout Sat. night I'll fly to Nashville to record a session on Sunday night at 8: P.m. Then I'll fly back home on Monday morning. Back

for the Apple Blossom Felestible here
on the 26th + 27th. I'll be here in
2 parades both days. There will
be movies made of this parade
far to go along with the news
reels.
at Theators around the country.
I'm sending in another pan.
My ex-band leader you know.
Well I must clos and get
ready to play tonight.

Write real soon and I'll be
seeing you on T.V. and write you
all about my trip later.

Tell Mary hello and if you
need any material for the club
let me know. Love always. Patsy.

April 18/56

Dear Treva:

    Just a line to say hello and hope this finds you in the pink.

    As for me I'm fine and as happy as if I had good sense. Ha.

    This Sat. night I'll be on the Jubilee. I'm leaving Fri. morning at 8: A.M. and after the show Sat. night I'll fly to Nashville to record a session on Sunday night at 8 P.M. Then I'll fly back home on Monday morning. Back for the Apple Blossom Festival here on the 26th and 27th. I'll be here in 2 parades both days. There will be movies made of this parade to go along with the news reels, at theaters around the country. I'm sending in another fan. My ex-band leader you know.

    Well I must close and get ready to play tonight.

    Write real soon and I'll be seeing you on T.V. and write you all about my trip later.

    Tell Max hello and if you need any material for the club, let me know.

                    Love Always, Patsy

Priv. 21

May 1, 56

Patsy Cline
Coral Recording Artist
Winchester, Virginia

Dear Treva:

Got your letter and was real glad to hear from you.

Got to Springfield last Fri. a week ago and Eddy Arnold met me at the air port. Went to rehersals Sat morning and met Bobby Lord, (a wonderfull person) Billy Walker, Wanda Jackson, Uncle Sipe, Marvin Rainwater. & all the folks on the Jubilee They are a real fine bunch of

4.

people. But I was supposed to
sing 2 songs but they didn't
have the right information on
it, so I didn't get to do but
one number. "Turn The Cards".

Went to Nashville on Sunday.
and had my session at 8. P.m on
Sunday night. And I'm real happy
with this one. Paul Cohen was
there and he says he's gonna
buy my contract from Coral
and put me on Decca. The
16th of June I go back to do
the T.V. show "Grande Ole Opry"
the Prince Albert portion this
time

Patsy Cline
Coral Recording Artist
Winchester, Virginia

Then Paul Cohen is gonna take me to New York do a recording session, with a 21 peice or-chestra and 15 peice male chorus to do "Just A Closer Walk With Thee" and "Lifes Railway To Heaven", and 2 others, but I'll find ~~2~~ new ones for the other one later on. But I'm *not* going pop. Just do these hymns with an orchestra. Paul says Red Foley sold ¾ million records of "Closer

IX.

Walk With Thee" and I can 8 million
of it, doing it my way & style.
I hope & pray that he's right.
The Apple Blossom was a big
susses. I got to sing for the
Queen & her court at the Queens
Ball. with Claude Thornhill &
his orchestra. So I've had a real
fine 5 days since I've got home.
And this past Sat. night on T.V.
with Jimmy Dean, they welcomed
me back on the Jamboree.
I'm working 5 nights a week now
and I'm busy as can be. but I

V.

Patsy Cline
Coral Recording Artist
Winchester, Virginia

wanted to write you to let you know how my trip was and how things were here at home.

You write real soon and tell me what the news is.

Tell Bruce & Max hello and good luck. I'm driving to Tenn in June I think so I might be able to stop in.

Write soon.
Love Always
Pat.

P.S. I'll send you some
pictures of the apple bloom
when I git them. They are
in color.

May 1, 56

Dear Treva:

Got your letter and was real glad to hear from you.

Got to Springfield last Fri. a week ago and Eddy Arnold met me at the airport. Went to rehearsals Sat morning and met Bobby Lord, (a wonderful person) Billy Walker, Wanda Jackson, Uncle Sipe, Marvin Rainwater, and all the folks on the jubilee. They are a real fine bunch of people. But I was supposed to sing 2 songs but they didn't have the right information on it, so I didn't get to do but one number, "Turn The Cards."

Went to Nashville on Sunday and had my session at 8:PM on Sunday night. And I'm real happy with this one. Paul Cohen was there and he says he's gonna buy my contract from Coral and put me on Decca. The 16th of June I go back to do the T.V. show Grand Ole Opry the Prince Albert portion this time. Then Paul Cohen is gonna take me to New York do a recording session, with a 21 piece Orchestra and 15 piece male chorus to do 'Just A Closer Walk With Thee" and " Life's Railway To Heaven," and 2 others, but I'll find 2 new ones for the other one later on. But I'm <u>not</u> going pop. Just do these hymns with an orchestra. Paul says Red Foley sold 4 million records of "Closer Walk With Thee" and I can 8 million of it, doing it my way and style. I hope and pray that he's right.

The Apple Blossom was a big success. I got to sing for the Queen and her court at the Queens Ball with Claude Thornhill and his orchestra. So I've had a real fine 5 days since I've got home.

And this past Sat. night on T.V. with Jimmy Dean, they welcomed me back on the Jamboree.

I' m working 5 nights a week now and I'm busy as can be, but I wanted to write you to let you know how my trip was and how things were here at home.

You write real soon and tell me what the news is.

Tell Bruce and Max hello and good luck. I'm driving to Tenn in June I think so I might be able to stop in.

Write soon.

Love Always,
Pat.

PS. I'll send you some pictures of the Apple Bloom when I get them. They are in color.

Bobby Lord, Billy Walker, Wanda Jackson, Uncle Sipe, and Marvin Rainwater were cast members of "Ozark Jubilee." Eddy Arnold had his own ABC television show filmed in Springfield.

•

Paul Cohen was Decca's A&R man. The two hymns he wanted her to sing, with an orchestra and chorus were recorded on July 2, 1959, in Nashville.

Patsy Cline
Coral Recording Artist
Winchester, Virginia

~~May~~ May 14/56

Dear Treva:

I got your letter today and was glad to hear from you again. Thought I'd drop you a line to say hello and that I'm still working.

The ole summer has hit at last here and today I dripped all day.

Went out to the Stock car races here in Winc. yesterday and did a personal appearance to about 3000 people. and it was soo-ooo hot.

Last Sat. nite for the first time

II.

I wore a blue & white western dress. Mom made it for me and every- one liked to had a fit over it. So this summer I'll do shows & T.V. work in western dress. I'm having pictures taken of it and I'll send you a copy soon. Inclosed is one of Jimmy Dean, Ted Mac & myself at W.M.A.L. television studio. Maybe you could use it in the write-ups. The little picture of you was good and I put it in my billfold. The Apple Blossom pictures didn't come out too good. They were'nt close up enough, but here's one and in the fall I'm getting this Oldsmobile. This is my blue suit with white stars in rhinestones on it. I think it's pretty. Well I must close & gett ready for my date. All my write soon. Love. Pat.

May 14, 56

Dear Treva:

I got your letter today and was glad to hear from you again. Thought I'd drop you a line to say hello and that I'm still working.

The ole summer has hit at last here and today I dripped all day.

Went out to the stock car races here in Winc. yesterday and did a personal appearance to about 3000 people, and it was soo-ooo hot.

Last Sat. nite for the first time I wore a blue and white western <u>dress</u>. Mom made it for me and everyone liked to had a fit over it. So this summer I'll do shows and T.V. work in western dress. I'm having pictures taken of it and I'll send you a copy soon. Enclosed is one of Jimmy Dean, Ted Mac and myself at W.M.A.L. television studio. Maybe you could see it in the write-ups.

The little picture of you was good and I put it in my billfold.

The Apple Blossom pictures didn't come out too good. They weren't close up enough, but here's one and in the fall I'm getting this Oldsmobile. This is my blue suit with white stars in rhinestones on it. I think it's pretty. Well must close and get ready for my date. All my love.

Write soon, Pat

Ted Mack was the host of the long-running, television show, "The Original Amateur Hour."

Patsy with recording artist Jimmy Dean, right, and Ted Mack, center, host of the popular television show, "The Original Amateur Hour."
From Treva's personal scrapbook, courtesy of Bruce Steinbicker.

PATSY CLINE

Hinakistey Va.
May 28/56

Dear Treva:

Got your most welcome letter and was happy to hear from you again.

Hope this finds you in the best of health and lucky in your living.

As for me I'm beginning to think I have no luck any more at just every day living. My ex husband is trying to cause me a lot of trouble because I won't fight the divorce, and I'm still having trouble with my car. I'm going to try & trade again soon.

As far as singing; everything is looking up. I just signed with Decca, and I'm nearly bustting with joy. On the 16th of June (of course I told you) I'll be on the Opry. Town & Country Jamboree just signed for 5 years & a net work (6 hours) is coming through also. I suppose you saw in the Jamboree magazine where the Disc Jockey poll of the

97

II

"Ten Top New Female Singers", I got No 3.
and in Country Song Round up, Jimmy
Rodgers Poll of the "Top Ten Female Singers"
I was No 7. I'm really happy about that
to.

There is a girl here in Washington who is
representative for Jim Dean and she wants
to be mine representative & get me more
numbers for our clubs. I told her I'd give
you her name & address & you two could
discuss it. So it's "Stoney Vigil."
1715 - 18th St. N. W.
Washington, 9, D.C.
She's a very kindly looking person
who looks like she just wants to be a
part of the music world so much, that
I believe she would be O.K. But you
sound her out Treva and see what you
think? Tell Bruce I'm so very sorry
I haven't answered his last letter. I feel
like a heel, but I don't get to even answer
my fans here hardly.

Well, my fellow (Charlie) is getting
me a diamond before long, and I'm so
happy, but we are getting to wait 12 mo's,

Winchester, Va.
May 28/56

Dear Treva:

Got your most welcome letter and was happy to hear from you again. Hope this finds you in the best of health and lucky in your living.

As for me I'm beginning to think I have no luck any more at just everyday living. My ex-husband is trying to cause me a lot of trouble because I won't fight the divorce, and I'm still having trouble with my car. I'm going to try and trade again soon.

As far as singing, everything is looking up. I just signed with Decca and I'm nearly busting with joy. On the 16th of June (of course I told you) I'll be on the Opry. Town and Country Jamboree just signed for 5 years and a net work (1 hour) is coming through also. I suppose you saw in the Jamboree magazine where the Disc Jockey poll of the "Ten Top New Female Singers," I got No 3, and in Country Song Roundup, Jimmy Rodgers Poll of the "Top Ten Female Singers" I was No 7. I'm really happy about that too.

There is a girl here in Washington who is representative for Jim Dean and she was to be my representative and get me more members for our club. I told her I'd give you her name and address and you two could discuss it. So it's "Stoney Vigil"

1715-18th St. N.W.

Washington, 9, D. C.

She's a very humble looking person who looks like she just wants to be a part of the music world so much, that I believe she would be O.K. But you sound her out Treva and see what you think? Tell Bruce I'm so very sorry I haven't answered his last letter. I feel like a heel, but I don't get to even answer my fans here hardly.

Well, my fellow (Charlie) is getting me a diamond before long, and I'm so happy, but we are going to wait 12 mo. to make sure. I feel like I'm sure now, for the first time in my life.

Well I must close and get some money orders off and more letters.

You write soon, and tell me all the news.

The negative you wanted is enclosed. I'm working on the "around home" pictures now.

Good luck and God Bless You.

Your Friend Always,
Patsy

PS. The News Letter No 1 is just fine. I'm real pleased with it. I'm mailing you an eight by ten picture this Fri. of the one I've been trying to get all along for real publicity. Enclosed are some names you can write to join my club.

In signing with Decca, Patsy was assured that her records would appear on the Decca label instead of its subsidiary, Coral.

•

Patsy met Charlie Dick on April 13 at a dance she performed at in nearby Berryville, Virginia

---

Patsy and Dale Turner backstage at "Town and Country."
From Treva's personal scrapbook, courtesy of Bruce Steinbicker.

July 20/56

Patsy Cline
Coral Recording Artist
Winchester, Virginia

Dear Treva.

Golly! gal I'm sorry I
haven't written to you in so
long. It looks like I just never
get a chance to write to any one
anymore. I'm working six days
a week and I've been going to
the Dr. He says I'm not getting
enough rest and he's going to
put me in bed about three
days a week or the hospital
if I don't slow down. I'm try-

4.

ing to fix up a three room apartment here at Mom's. Remodleing
painting and building more
to the rooms, so I can move
in befor cold wheather sets in.
Then I've got 3 mons. booked
in Florida (if I want it) start
ing in Sept, but the only reason
I'd go down there + work would
be to get a quicker "divorice"
than I'm getting now. I can get
one there in 3 mons. If the
pay is good I might take it,
In Miamie, Florida – Would
be nice wouldn't it? It would

111

Patsy Cline
Coral Recording Artist
Winchester, Virginia

he T.V. with Westley Tuttle and night clubs. I'm thinking about it. I'm signing "Connie B. Gay" as my personal manager + agent the first Aug. He wants me to go to Dallas Texas, Passadine Calif. + over seas, but I don't know. I've got work running out my ears.

Treva I'll send you the money Monday morning money order, + you let me know if I send you about 5 of my new records if you could use them? And

<u>IV</u>

I'm taking all my 8x10 pictures +
putting a lot of information on
the back of them and also where
they can write to you for my
Fan Club. I think you will
get some letters on this. Should
help raise my fan club members.
I sure wish we could get together and compare all the publicity and news items, D.J. letters
and pictures that I have. It
would help you. But I have it
all in one book.

How are you and Bruce? Tell
Max good luck + I said hello. I'll
write more later Baby. Write me
if you want to know any thing. Patsy
<u>Love</u>

July 20/56

Dear Treva:

Golly! gal I'm sorry I haven't written to you in soo long. It looks like I just never get a chance to write to any one anymore. I'm working six days a week and I've been going to the Dr. He says I' m not getting enough rest and he's going to put me in bed about three days a week or the hospital if I don't slow down. I'm trying to fix up a three room apartment here at Mom's. Remodeling, painting and building more to the rooms, so I can move in before cold weather sets in.

Then I've got 3 mons. booked in Florida (if I want it) starting in Sept. but the only reason I'd go down there and work would be to get a quicker divorce than I'm getting now. I can get one there in 3 mons. if the pay is good I might take it. In Miami, Florida. Would be nice wouldn't it? It would be T.V. with Wesley Tuttle and night clubs. I'm thinking about it. I'm signing Connie B. Gay as my personal manager and agent the first Aug. He wants me to go to Dallas Texas, Pasadena Calif. and overseas, but I don't know. I've got work running out my ears.

Treva, I'll send you the money Monday morning money order, and you let me know if I send you about 5 of my new records if you could use them? And I'm taking all my 8x10 pictures and putting a lot of information on the back of them and also where they can write to you for my Fan Club. I think you will get some letters on this. Should help raise my fan club members. I sure wish we could get together and compare all the publicity and news items, D.J. letters and pictures that I have. It would help you. But I have it all in one book. How are you and Bruce? Tell Max good luck and

106

I said hello. I'll write more later Baby. Write me if you want to know anything.

Love. Patsy.

"I've Loved and Lost Again." backed with "Stop, Look and Listen." was released on the Decca label on July 8, 1956.

•

Wesley Tuttle was best known as a performer and director of Town Hall Party, a California country music television show.

•

Patsy never signed Connie B. Gay as her manager

Patsy is introduced at the Disc Jockey Convention in 1956.
Courtesy of the Country Music Hall of Fame

.

Winchester Va
Aug 5th '56
Sun Morning

Dear Treva!

Well I suppose you are ready to
hang me by now and I wouldn't blame you
one bit. I'se just got the same old story and
it's true. Treva, honest I never get a minute to
my self any more. I think some times I'll flip
my lid if I don't get away from people. I get
soo sick of going, going, going, and when I do get
home to rest, in will come anywhere from 2 to 6
people just to be around enough so you have
to entertain them or lose friends, or then the
telephone stays hot.

I just got in from a 100 mile trip (200 round trip)
from 3 shows in Staunton, Va. I haven't had a
Sunday off for 3 months.

I know Bruce must think I'm a smart somebody. I never answered his two last letters, but
I'll try to in this letter.

Treva, I'm at long last sending the money.
I don't remember what the amount was anymore but I'm sending $6.00 if you need more
just say soo.

Another thing I want you to get in touch
with (Dale Turner, of Town & Country Time.
Capital Arena 14th + W. St.
Washington, D.C.
and tell her to give you all the information
on her so you can give her a story in my

journal. Her fan club pres. is putting her write up in her book on me, and givin your name to write to for joining the club, so I want you to do a little good for her too. She is a real sweet kid. She's not on records but she works every Sat night 3 hours T.V. with me on "Town & Country Time Jamboree. I'd love to help this kid in every way possible, It's a long & sad story behind it all and I'll tell you about her some time. She wants to be able to sing like me before she leaves this world. (Oh! she is well in health) but she knows and people all around her have made the mistake of telling her to "get a job at some thing she can do)". I think this is awfull. I've tried to help and encourage the girl, but she just sings out her ~~mou~~ nose too much. She says I've taught her a lot and she has at last got a set rage now for working on T.V. For a long time she worked for nothing just soo she could be part of the entertainment world.

Don't mention any of this. Just say you want to do a story. I'll tell you all about it some time. Brue Well Bruce, I thank you for your letters and I'm hoping you find a job before long and not to far away from Tres. She is a wonderfull person. I'm glad you can be down there with her. You both be good & write to me soon. Yours Friend Here is the blanks you wanted answered. Pat

Winchester, Va.
Aug. 5th/56
Sun. Morning

Dear Treva:

Well I suppose you are ready to hang me by now and I wouldn't blame you one bit. I've just got the same old story and it's true. Treva, honest I never get a minute to myself any more. I think sometimes I'll flip my lid if I don't get away from people. I get so sick of going, going, going, and when I do get home to rest, in will come anywhere from 2 to 6 people just to be around enough so you have to entertain them or lose friends, or then the telephone stays hot.

I just got in from a 100 mile trip, 200 round trip from 3 shows in Staunton, Va. I haven't had a Sunday off for 3 months.

I know Bruce must think I'm a smart somebody. I never answered his two last letters, but I'll try to in this letter.

Treva, I'm at long last sending the money. I don't remember what the amount was anymore but I'm sending $6.00 if you need more just say so.

Another thing I want you to get in touch with Dale Turner, c/o" Town and Country Time." Capital Arena 14th and W. St. Washington, D. C. and tell her to give you all the information on her so you can give her a story in my journal. Her fan club pres. is putting a big write-up in her book on me, and given your name to write to for joining the club, so I want you to do a little good for her too. She is a real sweet kid. She's not on records but she works every Sat night 3 hours T.V. with me on "Town and Country Time Jamboree." I'd love to help this kid in every way possible. It's a long and sad story behind it all and I'll tell you about her some time. She wants to be able to sing like me before she leaves this world. (Oh! she is well in health) but she knows and people all around have made the mistake of telling her to "get a job at something she can do." I think this is awful. I've tried to help and encourage the girl, but she just sings out her

111

nose too much. She says I've taught her a lot and so has at last got a set range now for working on T.V. For a long time she worked for nothing just so she could be part of the entertainment world.

Don't mention any of this. Just say you want to do a story. I'll tell you all about it sometime.

To Bruce Well Bruce, I thank you for your letter and I'm hoping you find a job before long and not too far away from Treva. She is a wonderful person. I'm glad you can be down there with her. You both be good and write to me soon. Here are the blanks you wanted answered.

Your Friend
Pat

Dale Turner never developed the singing career she hoped for.

•

Bruce found work at local radio station WEMB and later WETB.

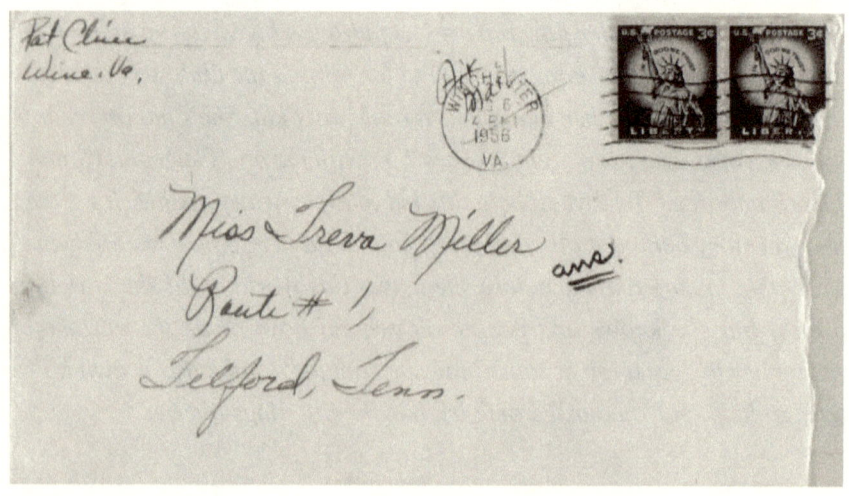

Winchester, Va
Sept 4/56

Dear Treva:

I'm sorry I haven't sent you any money or wrote to you befor now, but I've been trying to get a new costume together and trying to get ready for my trip to New York this Thursday. To try for the Aruther Godfrey Show on Mondays. The talent contest part you know? I've been trying to get there for a long time but I didn't get any where befor, this time I'll see what they think. If I get to go back, I'll let you know right away.

II.

Trva, a girl named ~~Joyce~~ Joan Dove, here in Winchester, called and wanted me to give her some entry blanks for the fan club, so I sent her all I had and she has signed up about a dozen members already and wants to do a lot of advertising on Fan Club for Patsy Cline. She has a lot of other girls helping her find new ~~customers~~ members.

I think if you help her with some information on how to get a sort of branch of the club here in my home town, it would help me and ~~both you~~ you both.

III.

Write to here, and get her some blanks to sign up more people.

She worries me to death with questions and I don't have any answers. I don't know too much about running a club, so you try to give her some information please.

How have you been and how is the family & Bruce? As far me I'm still working every day, some times two shows a day, and still not making too much money.

Well, I must close + I'll send you some money Fri. Sept 7th.

Oh! By the way Sept 8th I'll be 28 years old. I'm an old woman

4.

here already, & I feel like it
once in a while.

White real soon, & keep up
the good — Thanks for being
soo very patient with me.

Tell all hello and
be good.

Yours Always

Patsy Cline.

Winchester, Va
Sept 4/56

Dear Treva:

I'm sorry I haven't sent you any money or wrote to you before now, but I've been trying to get a new costume together and trying to get ready for my trip to New York this Thursday to try for the Arthur Godfrey Show on Mondays. The talent contest part you know? I've been trying to get there for a long time but I didn't get anywhere before, this time I'll see what they think. If I get to go back, I'll let you know right away.

Treva, a girl named Joan Dove, here in Winchester, called and wanted me to give her some entry blanks for the Fan club, so I sent her all I had and she has signed up about a dozen members already and wants to do a lot of advertising on Fan Club for Patsy Cline. She has a lot of other girls helping her find new members. I think if you help her with some information on how to get a sort of branch of the club here in my home town, it would help me and you both. Write to her, and get her some blanks to sign up more people.

She worries me to death with questions and I don't have any answers. I don't know too much about running a club, so you try to give her some information please.

How have you been and how is the family and Bruce? As for me I'm still working every day, sometimes two shows a day, and still not making too much money.

Well, I must close and I'll send you some money Fri. Sept 7th.

Oh! By the way Sept 8th I'll be 24 years old. I'm an old woman here already, and feel like it once in a while.

Write real soon and keep up the good and thanks for being so very patient with me.

Tell all hello and be good.

Yours Always,
Patsy Cline

The audition for Arthur Godfrey's show was not an apparent success. The producers were not particularly encouraging and although they told Patsy they would call her, she thought they were just being polite.

Sept 10/56.

Dear Treva:

I'm sending you the five
dollars you ask for and I just
got a little time here to thank
you for the lovely gift you +
the members sent. It's just lovely
and I'm real happy about it.

Thank them for me or send
me their addresses so I can
write them a note to thank them.

_11._

Honest, it is so pretty and I was soo surprised.

Mom gave me a dozen red roses and a wonderfull party yesterday. I got all kinds of pretty things and just had a wonderfull time. I'll write more later, got to go pay some bills now + go to the bank.

Write soon + thanks again for the gift and thank Bruce for the card. Tell him hello.

By for now. Love
Pat.

Sept 10/56

Dear Treva:

I'm sending you the five dollars you ask for and I just got a little time here to thank you for the lovely gift you and the members sent. It's just lovely and I'm real happy about it.

Thank them for me or send me their addresses so I can write them a note to thank them. Honest, it is so pretty and I was soo surprised.

Mom gave me a dozen red roses and a wonderful party yesterday. I got all kinds of pretty things and just had a wonderful time. I'll write more later, got to go pay some bills now and go to the bank.

Write soon and thanks again for the gift and thank Bruce for the card. Tell him hello.

Bye for now.

Love

Pat.

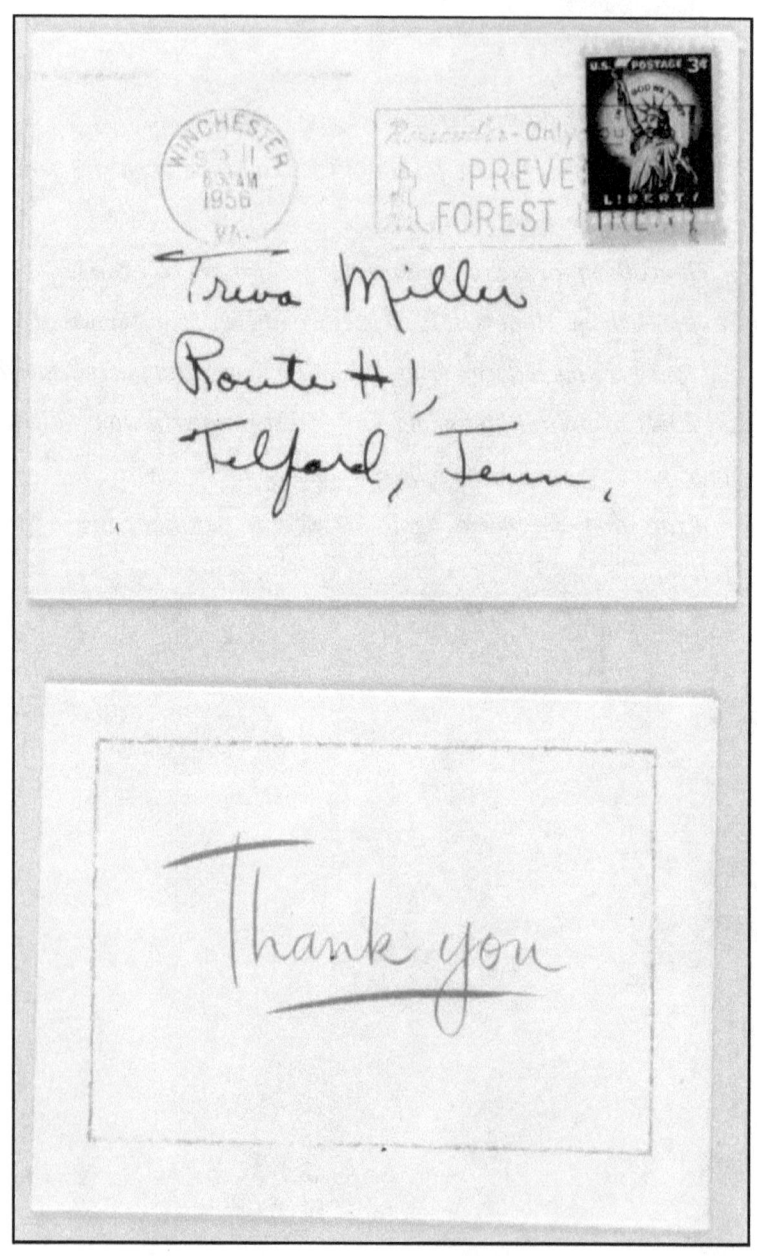

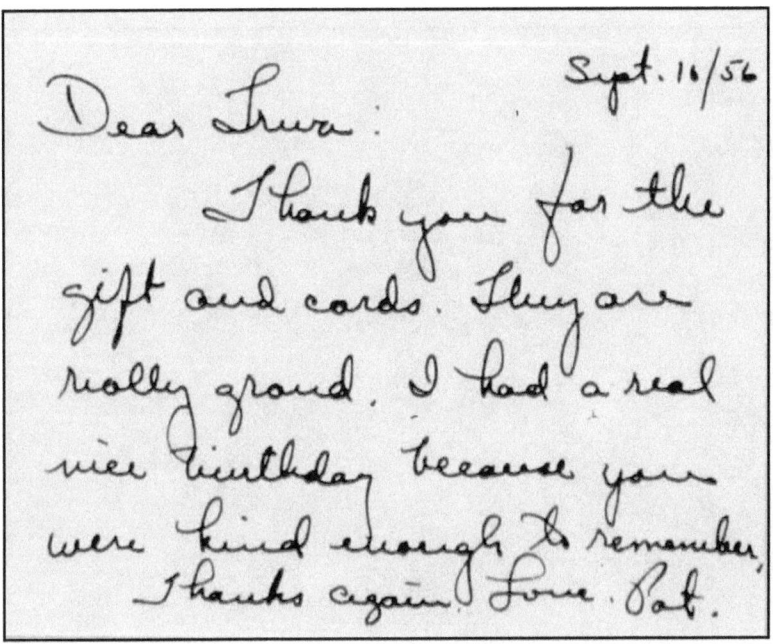

Sept. 10 / 56

Dear Treva:

Thank you for the gift and cards. They are really grand. I had a really nice birthday because you were kind enough to remember. Thanks again.

Love. Pat.

Winchester, Va
Sept 25/56

Dear Treva:

Well I've never been soo
thrilled in my life as I was when
I opened up the mail and found
my own journal, and to see
what a wonderfull job you all
have done. I think it is just
wonderfull. The pictures are good
and the write up are fine. I
didn't realize there was enough
news on me to make a book as
you all have done. Treva I think
you have done wonderfull, and
my thanks to you & Bruce can

II.

never be enough. Thank you soo
very much, and all those who
helped.

That was very good on Jimmy
Dean. I'm sure he will be tickled
pink. I'll see if I can't get you
a story and pictures of the whole
Town & Country Time Jamboree to put
in the next one and you can tie it
in with me working there with them.
Don't say any thing about this but
I got a letter from a friend of mine
at W. M. A. L. Television station who
has recomended me to the "Lawrence
Welks" show for a new show starting
Oct. 1st called "New Faces & Hit Tunes".

I+1.

He sent them a letter telling them
about me and, then they wrote him
back asking for a history on me and
my records, and pictures, and said
it would be T.V. Network coast to
coast. they would pay me for an
appearance and fair out & back. California
I just hope and pray that it comes
back saying I can come out, and
there is a chance for a regular job on
his show. Treva, I don't think I
could do a show if I would get
the chance, because I'd be soo excited
I couldn't do anything. Keep your
fingers crossed for me. I really
need the money now because last

wants to help it, and I appreciate
but I wish she wouldn't call
every day and write me letters two
and 3 times a week. If I thought
she was going to operate in a big
way or really do any good I
would help her if I knew what
to do. I hope you understand.

Well, I must get busy writing
to Betty Summers. I haven't wrote
to her for a long time and I feel
awful about it. I have to write
so much I get tired of it.

Again it was wonderful there
and thanks a million. I'll write you
up some "thank you" letters for the
next one.

Love
Patsy

127

Winchester, Va.
Sept 25/56

Dear Treva:

Well I've never been so thrilled in my life as I was when I opened up the mail and found my own Journal, and to see what a wonderful job you all have done. I think it is just wonderful. The pictures are good and the write up are fine. I didn't realize there was enough news on me to make a book as you all have done. Treva I think you have done wonderful, and my thanks to you and Bruce can never be enough. Thank you so very much, and all those who helped.

That was very good on Jimmy Dean. I'm sure he will be tickled pink. I'll see if I can't get you a story and pictures of the whole Town and Country Time Jamboree to put in the next one and you can tie it in with me working there with them.

Don't say anything about this, but I got a letter from a friend of mine at W.M.A.L. television station who has recommended me to the "Lawrence Welk" show for a new show starting Oct. 1st called "New Faces and Hit Tunes." He sent them a letter telling them about me and, then they wrote him back asking for a history on me and my records, and pictures, and said it would be T.V. network coast to coast, they would pay me for an appearance and fare out and back. (California.) I just hope and pray that it comes back saying I can come out, and there is a chance for a regular job on his show. Treva, I don't think I could do a show if I would get the chance, because I'd be so excited I couldn't do anything. Keep your fingers crossed for me. I really need the money now because last Thursday, I bought a new 56 Oldsmobile 88. I'm so tickled with it. I'm like a kid with a new toy.

Treva this Joan Dove is almost worrying me to death. She thinks I should tell her what to do and how and what she must do. See if you can't get her straightened out. She calls me every day nearly and wants me to come over and do write up for her, and I don't want to go out and do things like that. What little time I have I'd like it to be here at home. She's mad now because I won't come over to see her. Ha. Ha. If she writes, see if you can't get her straightened out. I know she wants to help and I appreciate but I wish she wouldn't call every day and write me letters two and 3 times a week. If I thought she was going to operate in a big way or really do any good I would help her if I knew what to do. I hope you understand.

Well, I must get busy writing to Betty Summers. I haven't wrote to her for a long time and I feel awful about it. I have to write so much I get tired of it.

Again it was wonderful Treva and thanks a million. I'll write you up some "thank you" letters for the next one.

Love
Patsy

Patsy never appeared on Lawrence Welk's show.

•

Both Joan Dove and Betty Summers were members of the Patsy Cline Fan Club.

Winchester, Va
Oct 8/56.

Dear Treva:

I'm sending you some
pictures and negatives for the
fan club books and you can
have them made up if you
wish. These don't look like
me I know, but this is the
way I'd look at home.

I'll only make this short now
because I'm on my way to Wash.
To design western costumes for
the "Prodner Hotel" for their
"Golden Steer Head" cocktail

lounge, and the waitresses
dress in little short western
costumes. I'm designing them
& Mom is making them, so
I'll write again this week
& try to answer Bruce's nice
little also.

If you need anything
more, let me know.

Bye now.
Love & Luck
Patsy

Winchester, Va.
Oct 8/56

Dear Treva:

I'm sending you some pictures and negatives for the fan club books and you can have them made up if you wish. These don't look like me I know, but this is the way I'd look at home.

I'll only make this short now, because I'm on my way to Wash. to design western costumes for the "Woodner Hotel" for their "Golden Steer Head" cocktail lounge, and their waitresses dress in little short western costumes. I'm designing them and Mom is making them, So I'll write again this week and try to answer Bruce's nice letter also.

If you need anything more, let me know.

Bye now.
Love and Luck
Patsy

Winchester, Va
Oct. 21/56

Dear Treva,

Just a little line or two to send you some information, some pictures, and some new items I would like in my next issue.

How are you and how is Bruce getting along? As for me I'm fine and trying to get things in shape to get ready for the D.J. convention. I'm going to the convention this year and I hope to see you & Bruce there. I'm going down on Tuesday, have a recording session on Wed. and go to the convention on Thurs, and I have to fly back to Richmond on Fri morning to play in Richmond Fri night. Then back to Wash. on Sat. for the Town + Country show.

-11-

Irene, These pictures I'm sending are of George Hamilton the IV. He's 18 years old, comes from North Carolina. Goes to college in Washington and last Monday night, was on the Godfrey show in N. York. He was on then the whole week. He is just wonderfull. He is a regular on Town & Country Jamboree and is on Colonial Records. His latest record is "A Rose & a Baby Ruth". & b/w. "If You Don't Know", George Hamilton The IV. He's been on the Grand Ole Opry on the Ernest Tubb show.

Dale Turner, you know her story I think. She appears on the Town & Country Jamboree every Sat. night.

Now don't let me forget to give you a story on Jimmy Dean & his Texas Wild Cats. Both of them this time. I'll send you a 8x10 pictures of the whole group. Then I have a picture of the new act on our show,

They are called "The Country Boys." Two boys who sound almost like the "Louvins", "Ira + Charlie". They are doing real well up here.

What I'm trying to do Irma is a story on the whole Town + Country Jamboree. I think with more pictures in this book it will be noticed more. What do you think."

Last night, I met "Mack", a fellow who use to play with Max. he says. Real nice fellow.

Inclosed are some small pictures of me in the dress. These negatives are in color I sent you.

Then I have a story I'm sending next week with the rest, on the other girl on our show. The "Little" "Lady" of Town + Country Jamboree "Miss Mary Flick". I'll send you her story along with the Cats.

I'll write my thank you letter + send it then. By now. Love Patsy.

Oct. 21/56

Dear Treva:

Just a little line or two to send you some information, some pictures, and some new items I would like in my next issue.

How are you and how is Bruce getting along? As for me I'm fine and trying to get things in shape to get ready for the D.J. convention. I'm going to the convention this year and I hope to see you and Bruce there. I'm going down on Tuesday, have a recording session on Wed. and go to the convention on Thurs., and I have to fly back to Richmond on Fri. morning to play in Richmond Fri. night. Then back to Wash. on Sat. for the Town and Country Jam.

Treva, these pictures I'm sending are of George Hamilton The IV. He's 18 years old, comes from North Carolina. Goes to college in Washington and last Monday night, was on the Godfrey show in New York. He was on then the whole week. He is just wonderful. He is a regular on Town and Country Jamboree and is on Colonial Records. His latest record is "A Rose and a Baby Ruth," and b/w, If You Don't Know." George Hamilton The IV He's been on the Grand Ole Opry on the Ernest Tubb show.

Dale Turner, you know her story I think. She appears on the Town and Country Jamboree every Sat. night.

Now don't let me forget to give you a story on Jimmy Dean + his <u>Texas Wild Cats</u> both of them this time. I'll send you a 8x10 picture of the whole group. Then I have a picture of the new act on our show. They are called "The Country Boys." Two boys who sound almost like the "Louvins," "Ira and Charlie." They are doing real well up here.

What I'm trying to do Treva is a story on the whole Town and Country Jamboree. I think with more pictures in this book it will be noticed more. What do you think.

Sat night, I met "Mack" a fellow who use to play with Max, he says. Real nice fellow.

Enclosed are some small pictures of me in the dress. These negatives are in color I sent you.

Then I have a story I'm sending next week with the rest, on the other girl on our show. The "Little" "Lady" of Town and Country Jamboree "Miss Mary Klick." I'll send you her story along with the Cats.

I'll write my thank you letter and send it then. Bye now.

Love, Patsy.

The DJ Convention was an annual festival held each November in Nashville to welcome disc jockeys to WSM and to treat them to a Grand Ole Opry show. Record companies and publishers hosted parties and award presentations. The event evolved into Country Music Week and is now CMA Festival.

•

Ira and Charlie Loudermilk, as the Louvin Brothers, debuted on the Grand Ole Opry in 1955. They were best known for their traditional bluegrass harmony vocals. Years later, Gram Parsons resurrected their work when he sang several of their songs with Emmylou Harris.

Winchester, Va
Nov. 18/56

Dear Treva;

I guess you are wondering where I've been for the past two or three weeks, so I thought I'd try to write a few lines to tell you all about my trip to Nashville last week and all about my four new recordings I just made.

Yes! I went to the D. J. convention and I had a ball. I mean a ball. Treva I never dreamed it was soo much fun. I had such a nice time. Bob Wills & his Texas Playboys played for the dance in the ball room of the Andrew Jackson Hotel and I went to the dance and after little Brenda Lee sang, they called on me, and I got the chance to sing with Bob's band and I don't think I ever had such a thrill except for the Opry.

At the recording session I cut these

songs. ④ "Pick Me Up On Your Way Down."
⑥ "A Poor Man's Roses or A Rich Man's Gold."
ⓒ "The Heart You Break May Be Your Own"
ⓓ Walkin After Midnight."

The one "Pick Me Up On Your Way Down." is the
only real cont country song I did this time.
And the one called "A Poor Man's Roses" is a
pop song but it's done with Hill billy music,
and they said I sound like Jo Stafford. All
of Decca's men were there and they all listen
to my session, and they said that this record
"Poor Man's Roses", & "Walkin After Midnight" will
be my hit record and that they are going to
push this one out like Presley was pushed.
And my bass man called the other day (Mr
McCall,) and he said he was talking to Kay
Starr in New York and she said there was
only one girl singer she feared and that was
Patsy Cline. Can you imagine that coming

139

III.

from Kay Starr' Treva? Maybe this one will
be my lucky break. I sure hope soo.

In this letter I'm sending you pictures of
our boy on Town & Country Time is George Hamilton
the IV. who sings "A Rose and a Baby Ruth". He
was on Steve Allens show tonight and his record
is #12 on the Nations top records now. He
is 18 years old, from N. Carolina, wrote the song
has a wonderfull personality and goes to college
in Washington. He's on our show every Sat.
night. So I'm sending you some pictures
of George & some of me by my self.

I talked with Bob Jennings while there in
Nashville, and he says he's been getting me
some fan s for my fan club. By the way,
Treva, if a girl named Margie Higgins writes
you for information on how to start a fan club
for the "Country Lads" who are on our show now,
They want to start a fan club for them-selves.
but they don't know anything about it. I'd
like for you to help them out if you will.

IV

Well, I guess I'd better close and you write and tell me whats new. I haven't heard from you for a spell.

I'll try to write you a letter for the journal Oh! I've got a weeks engagement at the Royal Casino in Washington. The finest night club in Wash. I'll take some pictures of us on stage.

Well, write soon Irene, & tell Bruce Hello.

By now & Love & Luck.

Patsy.

Winchester, Va.
Nov. 18/56

Dear Treva:

    I guess you are wondering where I've been for the past two or three weeks, so I thought I'd try to write a few lines to tell you all about my trip to Nashville last week and all about my four new recordings I just made.

    Yes! I went to the DJ convention and I had a ball. I mean a ball. Treva I never dreamed it was so much fun. I had such a nice time.

    Bob Wills and his Texas Playboys played for the dance in the ball room of the Andrew Jackson Hotel and I went to the dance and after little Brenda Lee sang, they called on me, and I got the chance to sing with Bob's band and I don't think I ever had such a thrill except for the Opry.

    At the recording session I cut these songs. (A.) "Pick Me Up On Your Way Down." (B.) "A Poor Man's Roses or A Rich Man's Gold." (C.) "The Heart You Break May Be Your Own" (D.) Walkin After Midnight."

    The one "Pick Me Up On Your Way Down." is the only real country song I did this time. And the one called "A Poor Man's Roses" is a pop song but it's done with Hillbilly music, and they said I sound like Jo Stafford. All of Decca's men were there and they all listened to my session, and they said that this record "Poor Man's Roses," and "Walkin After Midnight" will be my hit record and that they are going to push this one out like Presley was pushed.

    And my boss man called the other day, (Mr. McCall) and he said he was talking to Kay Starr in New York and she said there was only one girl singer she feared and that was Patsy Cline. Can you imagine that coming from "Kay Starr" Treva? Maybe this one will be my lucky break. I sure hope so.

    In this letter I'm sending you pictures of our boy in Town and Country Time, George Hamilton the IV, who sings "A Rose and a Baby Ruth." He was on Steve Allen's show tonight and his record is #12 on the nation's top records now. He is 18 years old, from N Carolina, wrote the song, has a wonderful personality and goes to college in Washington. He's on our show every Sat. night. So I'm sending you some pictures of George and some of me by myself.

I talked with Bob Jennings while there in Nashville, and he says he's been getting me some fans for my fan club. By the way, Treva, if a girl named Margie Higgins writes you for information on how to start a fan club for the "Country Lads" who are on our show now; they want to start a Fan club for themselves but they don't know anything about it.

I'd like for you to help them out if you will.

Well, I guess I'd better close and you write and tell me what's new. I haven't heard from you for a spell.

I'll try to write you a letter for the journal. Oh! I've got a week's engagement at the Royal Casino in Washington. The finest night club in Wash. I'll take some pictures of us on stage.

Well, write soon Treva, and tell Bruce hello.

Bye now and Love and Luck.

Patsy

Bob Wills and His Texas Playboys were some of the most influential country and western performers. Wills and his band were already known for their western swing, big band music. At the time Patsy sang with the band, they shared the same record label, Decca.

•

Brenda Lee was, at age eleven, a recording artist at Decca and a performer on television shows. She has had several hits on the pop and country charts and is now a member of the Country Music Hall of Fame.

•

Kay Starr and Jo Stafford were torch singers who enjoyed great success during the swing band era.

Treva, write up for Roy Acuffs journal.
Some thing else you
wanted I can't
remember what it was.

Patsy Cline
Coral Recording Artist
Winchester, Virginia

Hi There.

It sure is good to be able to talk to you wonderfull people once again, and to be a part of the Roy Acuffs journal.

I've worked with Roy and I must say, I've never worked with any one, so nice and soo considerate.

In my book, he is one of the best. I like his new recording out now with Kitty Wells, "Hello Mrs. Johnson."

I hope to able to work with you again soon Roy.

I'm going to the Opry in Oct. for another T.V. show coast to coast, + hope all you folks will be watching. I just hope to be able to meet all you nice people in person some time, and ~~that~~ you can get a copy of my new Decca Record called "I've Loved + Lost again". And if you ever get the chance, come to Wash. to see our "Town + Country Time Jamboree" over T.V. station W.M.A.L. Washington D.C. with Jimmy Dean + The Texas Wildcats. Hope to see you there.

By Now. Your Friend

Patsy Cline

Treva,- write-up for Roy Acuff's journal. Something else you wanted I can't remember what it was.

Hi There

It sure is good to be able to talk to you wonderful people once again, and to be a part of the Roy Acuff journal.

I've worked with Roy and I must say, I've never worked with any one, so nice and soo considerate.

In my book, he is one of the best. I like his new recording out now with Kitty Wells, "Hello Mrs. Johnson."

I hope to be able to work with you again soon Roy.

I'm going to the Opry in Oct. for another T.V. show coast to coast, and hope all you folks will be watching.

I just hope to be able to meet all you nice people in person some time, and that you can get a copy of my new Decca Record called "I've Loved and Lost Again." And if you ever get the chance, come to Wash. to see our "Town and Country Time Jamboree" over T.V station W.M.A.L. Washington D.C. with Jimmy Dean + The Texas Wildcats. Hope to see you there.

Bye now. Your Friend
Patsy Cline

Winchester, Va.
Nov. 19/56.

Dear Treva:

I have just tried to write you up a story to put in the journal. I hope you can make some sense out of it and get a story out of it.

There are a lot of mistakes, so see what you can do with it.

Use the pictures I sent you. and I think we will have a fine journal this time.

By the way Treva, can you find a place to make Xmas cards with my pictures on them? About 50 is all I need to send to the D.J.'s.

*If you need any more infor-
mation, write & let me know.
I'll say goodby for now.
Write real soon.*

*Love
Pat.*

Winchester, Va.
Nov. 19 / 56.

Dear Treva:

    I have just tried to write you up a story to put in the journal. I hope you can make some sense out of it and get a story out of it. There are a lot of mistakes, so see what you can do with it.

    Use the pictures I sent you, and I think we will have a fine journal this time.

    By the way Treva, can you find a place to make Xmas cards with my picture on them? About 50 is all I need to send to the DJs.

    If you need any more information, write and let me know.

    I'll say goodbye for now.

    Write real soon.

                       Love
                       Pat.

1957

Patsy was exhausted, not just from the busy holidays but from the demands of her career. "I've never been so sick of singing in my life," she says in her January 2 letter to Treva. She's been performing three shows a day, often as far as a hundred miles away from home. The travel is grueling, made even more so in one trip when she had to contend with two flat tires. To add to her frustration, she rarely finds peace at home. Either someone is at the door to see her, or the phone is ringing. For a brief moment Patsy thinks of leaving the business, but she can't afford to, even with as little money as she's making.

Fortunately, Patsy's despair is short-lived. Just a week later she announces the incredible news that she's been called to appear on Arthur Godfrey's Talent Scouts. With so much to do to get ready for the trip to New York, her note to Treva is brief. In fact, the next few letters to Treva are so short that the casual observer might not realize the import of that January 21 appearance. The truth is this one event was so obviously significant to Patsy that it didn't need explanation. It was the best thing that could possibly happen in her career. Even without today's hindsight, it was the defining moment in her move to stardom.

Patsy's performance was phenomenal. According to the show's format, each artist's presentation would be rated by the audience by way of a gimmick called the "applause meter." At the end of Patsy's song, the audience leapt to their feet to give her a standing ovation and the applause roared so loudly that the meter froze at its highest level. With this single performance Patsy's career was catapulted to a national level.

What is particularly interesting about Patsy's appearance on *Talent Scouts* is that she broke from tradition. Her opening number was the decidedly pop song "Walkin' After Midnight." She wore a sophisticated cocktail dress instead of the western clothes she was so fond of. Her choice of song and costume was on target. Winning *Talent Scouts* guaranteed her a place on Godfrey's morning radio show and she was asked to return to the television show the following week. It was almost unprecedented, but Godfrey liked her so well that he suggested that she return every six weeks to *his Arthur Godfrey and His Friends* show.

In all of Patsy's career, it seemed that as one opportunity presented itself another fell away. Now, it was time for Patsy to break from Connie Gay and "Town and Country." Gay believed Patsy was shunning him now that she'd moved up to the Godfrey show, but she honestly felt that Gay was not treating her fairly. In her letters to Treva she talked candidly about the split. By early March, Patsy is the center of a star-making whirlwind. Besides Godfrey's shows, she's recently been on the "Ozark Jubilee," the "Opry," and the "Town Hall Jamboree" in California. While there she did a speculative short film for Columbia to review. Everywhere speculation on Patsy's career was running high. There was talk of her appearing on nearly every major music variety show from Ed Sullivan's to Perry Como's. Some of these opportunities, such as the two just mentioned, never came to pass. Strangely, the most unlikely venue of all, Alan Freed's "The Big Beat" show, became a reality. Patsy's crossover appeal from a country to pop audience was complete.

Decca was anxious to capitalize on Patsy's newfound fame. Two recording sessions were scheduled in New York that April. Another was arranged in Nashville a month later. Enough songs were recorded to release an album. Patsy enlisted the help of her fan club in choosing the album's title. The member who submitted the name Patsy liked best, Patsy

Cline Sings, was awarded five dollars. Decca named the album simply Patsy Cline. It was released on August 5, 1957.

Three songs from the album were slated for singles: "Today, Tomorrow and Forever," "Three Cigarettes in an Ashtray, and "I Don't Wanta." In her letter to Treva, she called the last song "I Don't Wanna," however the Decca added the t to the record label. Not one of the songs charted, to say nothing of approaching the power of "Walkin' After Midnight." That record sold six hundred thousand copies within days of its release.

By November Patsy complained that she'd still not been paid for "Walkin' After Midnight." Bill McCall deducted every possible expense, from airfare to hotels, and when all the numbers were finally tabulated there was little left for Patsy's share of the royalties. After having a hit record, she was as broke as she'd ever been. Her career had swung like a pendulum and she was still not where she thought she would be. Her personal life was equally erratic because Charlie was drafted just weeks before her divorce from Gerald Cline became final.

Patsy and Charlie were married on September 15 in Winchester. Their love remained constant, but between Patsy's tour schedule and the U.S. Army's plans for Charlie they spent more time apart than they would have liked.

Patsy closed the year in Fayetteville, North Carolina, where Charlie was stationed. In her November letter to Treva, Patsy writes, "I need friends if I don't have anything else." For all the changes that the year had brought, so many things had stayed the same. Patsy had more success than she'd ever known, but she was still a long way from living the life of a star.

Winchester, Va
Jan. 2nd 57

Dear Treva,

I guess you think
I'm dead, but I'm almost
alive after this mess of
holidays. I'm soo sick of
people and telephone calls
I could scream. I've had to
work 14 days straight in a
row and every day some-
body either rings the door
bell or rings the phone
just as I try to get a little
rest. Honestly Treva, sometime I believe, If I was
out of debt, I'd just stop
singing all together. I've
never been soo sick of

II.

singing in my life, and the Dr. says I must take a vacation for 2 wks. But I can't afford to stop for 2 weeks. I think I would make out fine if I wasn't worried to death while I'm at home with phone calls & friends visiting. I don't mind friends, but I don't like them everyday. Then I'm a mess after all this 2 weeks of work. I can't even think good. I've been doing 3 shows a day.

About the pictures of George & I. I'm out. That was all I had then. I had

III.

about ten left + sold them
befor getting your letter.
I got a letter from the
boss yesterday and he
wants me to do an ~~alb~~
album. My "A Poor Man's
Roses or A ~~Rich~~ Man's ~~Gold~~"
will be out befor too long.
Every one here likes it +
thinks it will be the biggest
one yet.
And for the readers, you
can tell me them, if I do
start recording pop (which
I wouldn't like except I could
use the money) it will be
under the name of
"Ginny Patterson". Using
my middle name + first
name. That way no one

155

IV.

could put the 2 together
unless it was make public
public, What do you think
of the name?
Along with every thing else,
last Friday night I had
100 miles to go each way
to play and on the way down
to Fredericksburg I & blowed
the right front tire and
on the way back the left one.
So here goes $75.00 more.
I just give up.
Santa Clause was real
good to me. and I thank
you & the fan club members
for the wonderfull gifts.
The little pop-up toaster
was just soo cute. I showed
it to every one. Thanks soo

V,

very very much. I thank
each one of the members
by you writing a thank
you note on the typewriter
& I'll sign each letter
in my own writing. Will
you do this for me.
The name I picked
for the journal is (I think)
"Down The Trail With Patsy Cline" or
something like that. You'll
know which one I mean.
"Gunther Beer" renewed their
contract for Town & Country Time
again. Dale Turner, The Country
Lads "& "Elie Huston & Elmer
are going over seas in and
around the 17 of Feb.. Be
gone for 10 weeks. They
wanted me to go but I

VI

I can't leave home that long. Ha. I think I'll go on the Caribbian Tour for 10 days in July. instead.

Well I'll close for now. Be sending you some snap ~~shots~~ Shots befor long.

Happy New Year & tel all hello for me.

Tell Bruce I'll write to him when I get a little time to breath.

Be good & I'll be writing. Love

Patsy.

P.S.
By the way.
Dale isn't steading
for Nursery, She works
as secrytary for a Cat.
church. She is Cat.
~~—~~ tho.

PATSY CLINE

Winchester, Va.
Jan. 2nd/57

Dear Treva:

I guess you think I'm dead, but I'm almost alive after this mess of holidays. I'm so sick of people and telephone calls I could scream. I've had to work 14 days straight in a row and every day somebody either rings the doorbell or rings the phone just as I try to get a little rest. Honestly Treva, sometimes I believe, if I was out of debt, I'd just stop singing all together. I've never been so sick of singing in my life, and the Dr. says I must take a vacation for 2 wks. But I can't afford to stop for 2 weeks. I think I would make out fine if I wasn't worried to death while I'm at home with phone calls and friends visiting. I don't mind friends, but I don't like them everyday. Treva I'm a mess after all this 2 weeks of work. I can't even think good. I've been doing 3 shows a day.

About the pictures of George and I. I'm out. That was all I had then. I had about ten left and sold them before getting your letter.

Got a letter from the boss yesterday and he wants me to do an album. My "A Poor Man's Roses or A Rich Man's Gold" will be out before too long. Everyone here likes it and thinks it will be the biggest one yet.

And for the readers, you can tell them, if I do start recording pop (which I wouldn't like except I could use the money) it will be under the name of "Ginny Patterson." Using my middle name and first name. That way no one could put the 2 together unless it was made public. What do you think of the name?

Along with everything else, last Friday night I had 100 miles to go each way to play and on the way down to Fredericksburg I blew the right front tire and on the way back the left one. So here goes $75.00 more. I just give up. Santa Claus was real good to me, and I thank you and the fan club members for the wonderful gifts. The little popup toaster was just soo cute I showed it to everyone. Thanks soo very very much. I thank each one

159

of the members by you writing a thank you note on the typewriter and I'll sign each letter in my own writing. Will you do this for me?

The name I picked for the journal is (I think) "Down The Trail With Patsy Cline" or something like that. You'll know which one I mean. "Gunther Beer" renewed their contract for Town and Country Time again. Dale Turner, The Country Lads and "Elie Huston and Elmer" are going over seas in and around the 17 of Feb. Be gone for 10 weeks. They wanted me to go but I can't leave home that long. Ha. I think I'll go on the Caribbean Tour for 10 days in July instead.

Well I'll close for now. Be sending you some snapshots before long.
Happy New Year and tell all hello for me.
Tell Bruce I'll write to him when I get a little time to breathe.
Be good and I'll be writing.

Love
Patsy

P.S. By the way. Dale isn't studying for nunnery. She works as secretary for a Cat. church. She is Cat tho.

Patsy never recorded using the name Ginny Patterson.

•

After a fan club contest, Patsy chooses the name "Down the Path with Patsy Cline" among the several submitted by her members for the club journal.

Jan 9/57

Dear Treva,

Just got a call from Hodges and I leave the 17th of Jan. far to be on the Monday night show on the 21st of Jan. Mom is my scout I think. I'll be wearing a black & white suit. Thought I'd let you know. I'll send you the money as soon as possible. I'll try to get the letter wrote for the journal this week. Got soo much to do, and no money far a week in New York. Write soon & wish me luck.

Love Always. Patsy,

Jan 9 / 57

Dear Treva:

Just got a call from Godfrey and I leave the 17th of Jan. for to be on the Monday night show on the 21st of Jan. Mom is my scout I think. I'll be wearing a black and white suit.

Thought I'd let you know, I'll send you the money as soon as possible. I'll try to get the letter wrote for the journal this week. Got so much to do, and no money for a week in New York.

Write soon and wish me luck.

Love Always,
Patsy.

Every contestant on "Arthur Godfrey's Talent Scouts" show had to be accompanied by a "talent scout" to introduce the artist to Arthur Godfrey. This was usually not a family member but because Patsy and her mother used different last names, they were able to sidestep the rules.

Jan 17/57

Dear Treva,

Here is the journal letter. Hope you can get some sence out of it because I had to do a rush job. I can't hardly think right now in all this mess. I'll send you the $10.00 next Tuesday. That the best I can do. Re-write any thing you want in this letter.

By now. Love

Patsy -

Jan 17 / 57

Dear Treva:

Here is the journal letter. Hope you can get some sense out of it because I had to do a rush job. I can't hardly think right now in all this mess. I'll send you the $10.00 next Tuesday. That's the best I can do.

Re-write anything you want in this letter.

Bye now.

Love

Patsy

Hello again:

Well another year is past and a new year is born, and I know I'm a little late but a happy new year to everyone. I just hope everyone will have a successful year including myself. Ha, ha.

By the time you read this letter I'll be back from the big city of New York, but right now I'm getting ready to go. I'm leaving the 18th and I'll be on the Godfrey Talent Show, Monday the 21st. I really don't think I'll win but anyway I can say I've been there. My mother is going to be my scout. Right off hand I don't know of anyone who knows me better.

My new record is out and last Sat. night a DJ told me that in the top 50 country and western hits across the nation, (in Billboard) I last week was #48. And this week I am #42. That is the record "I've loved and Lost Again." I just hope my new record of "A Poor Man's Roses" picks up and keeps me going to that top 10. But I owe it to my fans and friends and I'm not forgetting that.

Well we have the journal and I want to thank the person who sent in the winning name. It was hard to pick because everyone had good ideas.

I hope everyone will like the pictures in the issue, because I think it makes the book more interesting. Let me know how you like the picture story idea.

This past Sat. night I had a long talk with Eddy Arnold. He was the guest on T.V. with us. He is the greatest when it comes to singing, but I don't agree with his ideas of getting on top. He says, "I could kinda go to the pop-side to please the public to get going and then do whatever I wanted."

I said "Eddy, I can't be something I'm not and the public will have to like me like I am." Am I right or wrong?

We took some pictures of the "Plow-boy" and myself. As soon as I get them made I'll send them on to you.

Well, The Country Lads, Dale Turner and Elie and Elmer from Town and Country Jamboree are going overseas for 10 weeks leaving in Feb. They are going to Africa, France and the Philippines. Let's wish them good luck and hope they have a good trip.

I want to thank everyone who gave me the much needed Christmas present. It was really nice and really cute. Also thanks to Treva for the salt and pepper shaker in the style of a pop-up toaster. I thank all of you very much.

I guess I better close and get busy packing for this city trip. Thanks again for the Xmas cards and letters. Bye for now.

Musically your Friend

The Tennessee Plowboy, Eddy Arnold, had a career that lasted more than fifty years. In the 1950s he did change his recording and stage style to appeal to a more sophisticated audience.

WESTERN UNION TELEGRAM

Springfield Mo. Feb 9 11:59 AM.

Miss Treva Miller
Route 1 Telford Tenn.

Ozark Jubilee tonight. California next week.

Love,
Patsy Cline.

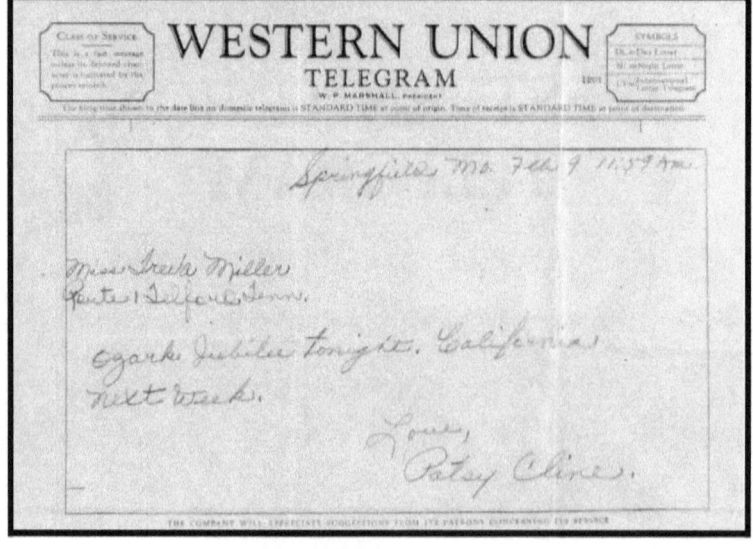

On The Plane. 9000ft. up.
Sun. 10/57

Hi Gal:

I sent you a telegram yesterday morning telling you I was on Jubilee but I know you didn't get it in time. Going to the Jubilee again March 2nd. In between I'm going to Town Hall, Calif. 22- 23rd.

Ed Sullivan show coming up in 5 weeks. Go back to Godfrey when he gets back from Africa. Then I'll be regular on Ozark Jubilee 2 Sat.s a month. They want me regular. I won't be at Town and Country anymore. I'll write and send you money tomorrow A.M.

Love. Patsy

Record has sold over 200,000. I can't believe it.

Patsy never performed on "The Ed Sullivan Show."

•

Some sources have stated that "Walkin' After Midnight" was released on February 11, 1957.

•

In this postcard, postmarked February 11, Patsy brags that the record has already sold 200,000 copies.

170

2/12/57

Dear Rina;

Just a card to let you know I'll be on my way to Nashville tonight and might stay over Sat night + the Opry wants me to stay on with them. Going to make some interview tapes with Nashville D.J's while I'm there.

Write again soon,

By now. Patsy.

2/12/57

Dear Treva:

    Just a card to let you know I'll be on my way to Nashville tonight and might stay over Sat. night and the Opry wants me to stay on with them. Going to make some interview tapes with Nashville DJs while I'm there.

    Write again soon.

    Bye now.

                                   Patsy.

From Treva's personal scrapbook, courtesy of Bruce Steinbicker.

P.S. Going home to-
night early (Sat) so
I can be with Charlie
He leaves in so days.

Nashville
2/16/57

Dear Treva,

Just wanted to say
hello and hope you got
the chance to hear me
+ Tom Perryman at W.S.M.
the other night. Looks like
my plans for moving to
Ozark are changed. I'm
coming to the Opry April
1st for P.A. slow try to move.
My Charlie has been called
to the D—— army. I just wish
I could die, Treva I cant
live with him not around.
Send a issue of journal to
Fred UpDyke, % of me at home.
I'll send $1.00 when I get home.
I'll write you. Leave for Calif.
Wed. Love, Patsy

P.S. Going home tonight early (Sat.) so I can be with Charlie. He leaves in 20 days.

Nashville
2/16/57

Dear Treva:

Just wanted to say hello and hope you got the chance to hear me and Tom Perryman at W.S.M. the other night. Looks like my plans for moving to Ozark are changed. I' m coming to the Opry April 1st for P.A. show and try to move.

My Charlie has been called to the D--army. I just wish I could die. Treva, I can't live with him not around.

Send an issue of journal to Fred Updyke, c/o me at home. I'll send $1.00 when I get home. I'll write you. Leave for Calif. Wed.

Love.
Patsy C.

Tom Perryman was then the all-night disc jockey at WSM. Because the station was a 50,000-watt clear channel, its radio programs could be heard for hundreds of miles, especially at night, and was very influential among, country music listeners.

2/27/59

Dear Treva:

I guess you think I'm never going to let you know where and what I'm doing. It's all so much to tell, but I'll try to write a few lines anyway. After the Godfrey show I came home and went to the Ozark Jubilee then to Nashville. Then I was out to California for the Town Hall Jamboree, and I did a short musical movie for Columbia to renew. This coming Sat, I go to Moleine, Ill. for a show, then back to California for these shows.

II.

The Tenn. (Ernie Ford daily) show, the Art Linkletter show, and the Bob Crosby show + Town Hall Party again, Then after that on to Nashville for the Opry on Sat night of March 15th (I think) and then to Knoxville for a show on Tenn. Barn Dance if they will take my price, then to the Ed Sullivan Show in New York, while there I'll do a recording session for one single record + 10 sides for an album.

When Mr. Godfrey get's back from Africa I'll be on his show, one week out of every six weeks, Then on to the Steve Allan + Perry Como shows so they say.

III.

Trevar, thank all these wonderful people for me that are writing to me, I just can't get the time out to write each one of them. I just never received such letters in my life. I just set right down + cry every time I get a big pile of them.

If you need any thing write to me + Mom will take care of you for me. Getting some new pictures made + Mom is making some new ~~western~~ dressey-dresses. I'm quit the Town + Country. They made a hate-ful dig at me on T.V. for

IV

not signing a contract to stay on the show here after winning on the Godfrey. So I just quit. I'm thinking of going to the Opry along about April 1st if they get straight down there at Nashville.

Well I must close + get things ready to go again.

Want to see you at the Knoxville Barn Dance if I come. I'll let you know when. Write soon + tell Bruce hello. My record is 17 in the top of field. Love

Patsy.

2/27/57

Dear Treva:

I guess you think I'm never going to let you know where and what I'm doing. It's all so much to tell, but I'll try to write a few lines anyway.

After the Godfrey show I came home and went to the Ozark Jubilee. Then to Nashville. Then I was out to California for the Town Hall Jamboree, and I did a short musical movie for Columbia to review. This coming Sat. I go to Moline, Ill. for a show, then back to California for these shows. The Tenn. Ernie Ford (daily) show, the Art Linkletter show, and the Bob Crosby show and Town Hall Party again. Then after that on to Nashville for the Opry on Sat night of March 15th (I think) and then to Knoxville for a show on Tenn. Barn Dance, if they will take my price, then to the Ed Sullivan Show in New York, while there I'll do a recording session for one single record and 10 sides for an album. When Mr. Godfrey gets back from Africa I'll be on his show, one week out of every six weeks. Then on to the Steve Allen and Perry Como shows so they say.

Treva, thank all these wonderful people for me that are writing to me, I just can't get the time out to write each one of them. I just never received such letters in my life. I just sit right down and cry every time I get a pile of them.

If you need anything write to me + Mom will take care of you for me. Getting some new pictures made + Mom is making some new western dressey-dresses. I've quit the Town and Country. They through a hateful dig at me on T.V. for not signing a contract to stay on the show here after winning on the Godfrey. So I just quit. I'm thinking of going to the Opry along about April 1st if they get straight down there at Nashville.

Well I must close and get things ready to go again. Want to see you at the Knoxville Barn Dance if I come. I'll let you know when.

Write soon and tell Bruce hello. My record is 17 in the pop field.

Love
Patsy.

Patsy did not perform on Steve Allen's, Perry Como's, or Art Linkletter's show. She may have performed on "The Tennessee Ernie Ford Show," a country music variety show on NBC, at a later date.

•

Patsy's departure from "Town and Country" was bitter. This marked the end of her association with Connie B. Gay, the man who only a year before had given her her big break in country music television.

Winchester, Va
3/7/57.

Dear Treva:

Thought I'd drop you
a few lines this wet shining
blue old night. I'm soo lonesome + sick at heart I could
die. My Charlie left Monday
and is in South Carolina now
but might go on to Fort Benning
Georgia Monday. I feel like my
arms are cut off. Treva, I've never
loved a man soo much in my
life. He is my life, my world,
just my everything. I guess
you think I'm nuts? But
I have to tell some body.
Other than this I'm in fine
health, + working as hard as

II

I can.

You ask how many records I had sold? Well as far as I knew 2 weeks ago we had sold 600,000 and was still selling 40,000 a day. Decca said I had already become their no 1. seller over Jerry Lewis, The Platters, and Bill Haley. Which made me feel proud. So if what they say is so, we should sell that million before long so I can get that gold record. I sure hope so.

Treva I'm sending a bunch of letters from fans wanting pictures & wanting to start fan club or where is mine so they can join? So write these folks for me & give them the info

Here is a listing of what I'll be
doing the next couple of months.
13th to 19th of March. California
for Bob Crosby, Art Linkletter Party,
Town Hall Party, & maybe Tenn. Ernie.
24th of March. Des Moines, Iowa,
with Webb Pierce, for big show.
27th March. Show for Red Cross
of Winchester.
April 1st supposed to be on the
Godfrey show but already have
the Opry April 1st if Godfrey
comes up the second week in April.
Got a session also first week in
April. for 1 single record + album.
The 18th to 24th of April, 2 weeks
on Broadway at the Paramount Theater
for a Rock + Roll show in New York
And I can get the Sullivan show
+ Perry Como show anytime I
get time

184

P.S. Last Sat. I did a show with Johnny Cash — Hank Shepard + Benny Martin. I got top billing. How about that?

Now! all we need is a new record. and one that is good. "Good." Ha

Mr. McCall is trying to put me back on Town & Country here in Washington. But after the dig they gave me on T.V. Sat. the 2nd, I will not go back unless Connie B. Gay (the boss) + Jane Simms (his secretary) apologize and give me $700.00 a week. They need a girl singer and can't find one good enough to put on his new C.B.S. T.V. show coast to coast (every morning) at 7 A.M. So when he gives me $700.00 per week for 5 days a week and $300.00 on Sat. nights, I'll go back. The union scale is $1,050.00 per week for that much work.

But I know he will have a fit
when he hears what I'm asking.
But I don't care. It's true,
his show was one step up, but
he could have showed a little
more appreciation for all the
publicity I gave his show and
have been doing in all my
fan club letters & could have
paid scale to me anyway.
He got mad because I wouldn't
sign a per. management contract
with him. He wanted 50%. How
about that ??

Treva, put me in any story book
you can find. It's O. K. with
me. T.V. Guide is doing a real
big story on me in April. I'll send
you a copy, I'll have new

Winchester, Va.
3/7/57

Dear Treva:

Thought I'd drop you a few lines this wet raining blue old night. I'm so lonesome and sick at heart I could die. My Charlie left Monday and is in South Carolina now but <u>might</u> go on to Fort Benning Georgia Monday. I feel like my arms are cut off. Treva, I've never loved a man so much in my life. He is my life, my world, just my everything. I guess you think I'm nuts? But I have to tell somebody.

Other than this I'm in fine health, and working as hard as I can.

You ask how many records I had sold? Well as far as I knew 2 weeks ago we had sold 600,000 and was still selling 40,000 a day. Decca said I had already become their No. 1 seller over Jerry Lewis, The Platters, and Bill Haley, which made me feel proud. So if what they say is so, we should sell that million before long so I can get that gold record. I sure hope so.

Treva, I'm sending a bunch of letters from fans wanting pictures and wanting to start fan club or where is mine so they can join? So write these folks for me and give them the info.

Here is a listing of what I'll be doing the next couple of months.

13th to 19th of March. California for Bob Crosby, Art Linkletter Party, Town Hall Party and maybe Tenn. Ernie.

24th of March. Des Moines, Iowa, with Webb Pierce for big show.

27th March. Show for Red Cross of Winchester.

April 1st <u>supposed</u> to be on the Godfrey Show but already have the Opry April 1st if Godfrey comes up the second week in April.

Got a session also first week in April for 1 single record and album.

The 18th to 28th of April, 2 weeks on Broadway at the Paramount Theater for a Rock and Roll Show in New York. And I can get the Sullivan Show and Perry Como Slow anytime <u>I get time</u>.

PS. Last Sat. I did a show with Johnny Cash and Jean Shepard and Benny Martin. I got top billing. How about that?

Now! All we need is a new record and one that is good. "Good" Ha.

187

Mr. McCall is trying to put me back on Town and Country here in Washington. But after the dig they gave me on T.V. Feb. the 2nd, I will not go back unless Connie B. Gay (the boss) and Jane Trimner (his secretary) apologize and give me $700.00 a week. They need a girl singer and can't find one good enough to put on his new C.B.S. T.V. show coast to coast (every morning) at 7:A.M. So when he gives me $700.00 per week for 5 days a week and $200.00 on Sat nights, I'll go back. The union scale is $1,050.00 per week for that much work. But I know he will have a fit when he hears what I'm asking. But I don't care. It's true, his show was one step up, but he could have showed a little more appreciation for all the publicity I gave his show and have been doing in all my fan club letters and could have paid scale to me any way. He got mad because I wouldn't sign a per. [percentage] management contract with him. He wanted 50%. How about that??

Treva, put me in any story book you can find. It's O.K. with me. TV Guide is doing a real big story on me in April. I'll send you a copy. I'll have new pictures this weekend and send you some of them. I'm having new and different clothes made. Dresses with sweet heart neck-line, ¾ in. sleeves with a big cuff on them, made princess style dress and 4 in. leather fringe in silver off the neck line and around the bottom of the skirt with music notes in silver all over it with rhinestones around fringe and notes. This way I can wear it in the semi-pop field and still be dressed up or in the country field. Treva I still can't believe it's all happened to me. Thank the folks for me and tell Bruce hello.

Write real soon.
Love Patsy.

Webb Pierce was one of the most successful country performers in the 1950s and 1960s and was known for his distinctive honky-tonk songs.

•

At the time she performed with Johnny Cash he was a Sun Records artist out of Memphis just making, his mark in country music.

•

Jean Shepard recorded for Capital Records at the time. Jean later married fellow Grand Ole Opry member Hawkshaw Hawkins, who would die with Patsy in the March 5, 1963, plane crash.

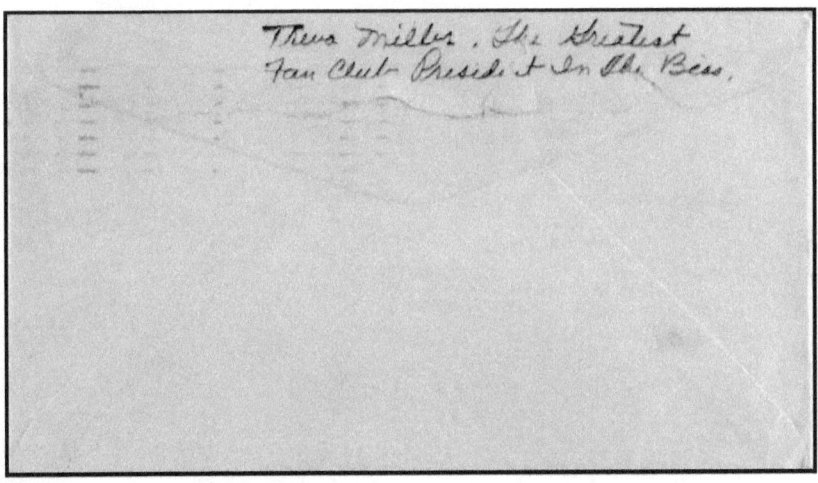

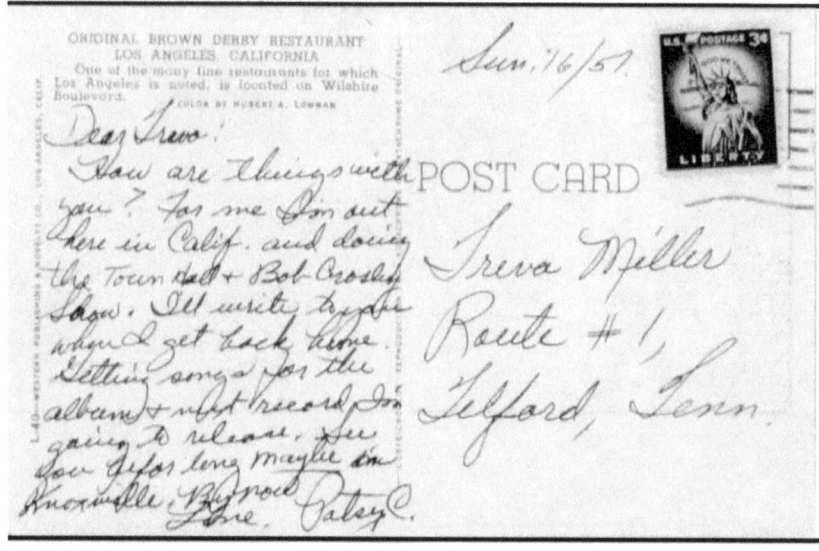

Sun. 16/57

Dear Treva:

How are things w ith you? For me I'm out here in Calif. And doing the Town Hall and Bob Crosby Show. I'll write to you when I get back home. Getting songs for the album and next record I'm going to release. See you before long maybe in Knoxville. Bye now.

Love, Patsy C.

According to the *Winchester Star* April 4, 1957, edition, Patsy appeared on "The Bob Crosby Show" on March 14. Bob, the younger brother of Bing Crosby, was an orchestra leader and singer. He hosted a musical variety show sometimes carried by the NBC network.

Winchester, Va
July 31/57

Dear Treva:

Well, I received your
letter and I'm sorry I have-
int written sooner, but I
had to take a little rest &
then I had to go to New York
for the "Big Beat" Show, which
I don't know if you seen or
not, last Fri. Then Aug 10th
I'm on the Ozark Jubilee again.
My Album is out and a new
single record "Three Cig In An Ash-
Tray" this coming Monday. They
are puting out a L.P. & and
an E.P. you know & songs on a
forty-five speed. So maybe
we will have good luck if

II.

some sort of out of 13 songs.
I sure hope so. Sure is a
bad time of the year right
now. The work is really
slowing down. All the Opry
acts are out hunting work.
So it's not only me that's
slowing down. The Ozark Jub.
is bidding on a new A.B.C. net
work show and if they get set
I'm suppose to work with
them on it.
How are you & the family?
Tell them all "hello" and
tell Bruce also "hello" and I
think he is a great guy. I
sure ug enjoyed talking to
you both at the Home coming
and it was such a trill

II -

to meet you both. I was never so surprised in all my life to see you all sitting there. But it was wonderful. You ask for some money, & I'll try to give you twenty dollars now and after I receive my check this Sat I'll send you $20.00 more, for the months I've skipped paying you. You could help me by writing me & letting me know I've missed your $10.00 each month when I miss Treva. I have so much Tess. to take care of.

If You want any 8x10 pictures just let me know. I got 500 more. I've got a lot of

IV.

letters to answer which I'm
sending to you. Lot just
want pictures.

Well, I must close and
get busy packing to leave
with Charlie this Mon. week for
North Carolina to look for
an appartment or trailer so
I can move the first of Sept.
Then next Fri. the 9th
I'll leave for the Ozark Jubilee
Then my next stop is the
Wisconsin State Fair in Wis.
for 9 days, then to Miss-
issippi Fair with Eddy Arnold.

And our house warming is
Aug. 29, 30. + 31.st, so I hope
on your trip you can stop by

V.

while the house warming is going on. I hope so that you must stop. I'll be home from the State Fair the 26th and you can stop on the 29th or 30th.

Well I must stop this time and get this off in the mail. Write real soon.

and I'll be looking for you both.

Love Always
Patsy.

Winchester, Va.
July 31/57

Dear Treva:

Well, I received your letter and I'm sorry I haven't written sooner, but I had to take a little rest and then I had to go to New York for the "Big Beat" Show, which I don't know if you seen or not, last Fri. Then Aug. 10th I'm on the Ozark Jubilee again.

My album is out and a new <u>single</u> record "Three Cigs In An Ash-Tray" this coming Monday. They are putting out an L.P. and an E.P. you know 4 songs on a forty-five speed. So maybe we will have good luck of some sort out of 13 songs. I sure hope so. Sure is a bad time of the year right now. The work is really slowing down. All the Opry acts are out hunting work. So it's not only me that's slowing down. The Ozark Jub. is bidding on a new A. B.C. network show and if they get it, I'm supposed to work with them on it.

How are you and the family? Tell them all "hello" and tell Bruce also "hello" and I think he is a great guy. I sure enjoyed talking to you both at the Homecoming and it was such a thrill to meet you both. I was never so surprised in all my life to see you all sitting there. But it was wonderful.

You ask for some money, and I'll try to give you twenty dollars now and after I receive my check this Sat I'll send you $20.00 more for the months I've skipped paying you. You could help me by writing me and letting me know I've missed your $10.00 each month when I miss Treva. I have so much biss. to take care of.

If you want any 8x10 pictures just let me know. I got 500 more. I've got a lot of letters to answer which I'm sending to you. Lot just want pictures.

Well, I must close and get busy packing to leave with Charles this Mon. week for North Carolina to look for an apartment or trailer so I can move the first of Sept. Then next Fri. the 9th I'll leave for the Ozark Jubilee.

Then my next stop is the Wisconsin State Fair in Wis. for 9 days, then to Mississippi Fair with Eddy Arnold.

And our house warming is Aug 29, 30, and 31st, so I hope on your trip you can stop by while the house warming is going on. I hope so, but you must stop. I'll be home from the State Fair the 26th and you can stop on the 29th or 30th.

Well I must stop this time and get this off in the mail.

Write real soon and I'll be looking for you both.

Love Always

Patsy

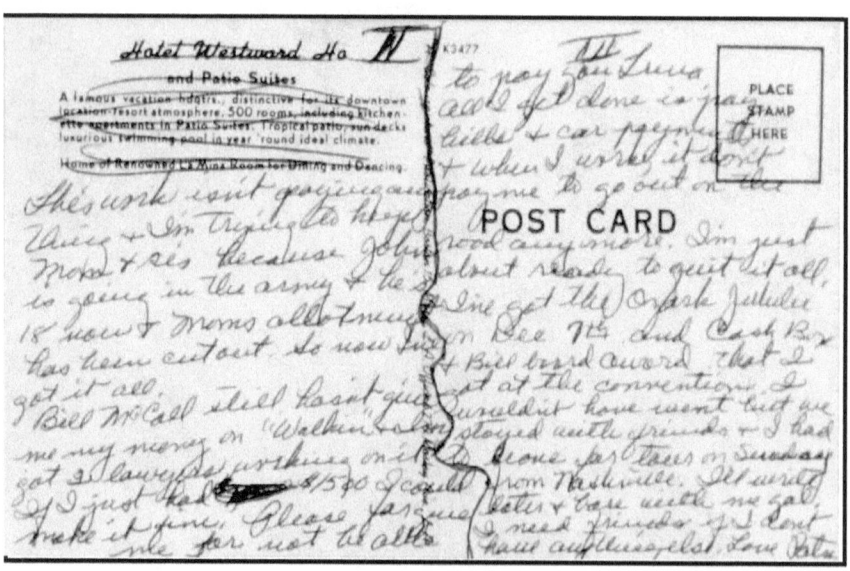

Address.
758 Poole Drive
Fayetteville, N.C.

Dear Treva:

I'm in Phoenix, Ariz. and got a week to go out yet and they got "I Don't Wanna" out on single, it's moving slow but moving. Yes I was on G. show 2 weeks ago. I didn't know it till Mon. and went up on Tues. The Xmas cards, you better leave alone, I'm out of money and you are due money now, so I'll try to send you at least $50.00 before long. Treva, I'm up to my neck and work is not doing anything. I'm trying to get things paid and nothing is working out.

This work isn't paying anything and I'm trying to keep Mom and sis because John is going in the army and he's 18 now and Mom's allotment has been cut out. So now I've got it all.

Bill McCall still hasn't give me my money on "Walkin." I've got 2 lawyers working on it. If I just had $1500 I could make it fine. Please forgive me for not being able to pay you Treva. All I get done is pay bills and car payments and when I work it don't pay me to go out on the road any more. I'm just about ready to quit it all. I've got the Ozark Jubilee on Dec. 7th and Cash Box and Billboard Award that I got at the convention. I wouldn't have went but we stayed with friends and I had to leave for tour on Sunday from Nashville. I'll write later and bear with me gal. I need friends !f I don't have anything else.

Love Patsy

The "G. Show" is probably her shorthand for "The Arthur Godfrey Show." She performed on October 25.

•

Patsy's younger brother, Samuel Laurence, was called John by the family.

1958

In January, long before she shared her news with the rest of the world, Patsy told Treva that she was pregnant. As it turns out, she couldn't have chosen a better time to slow her career because the country music field entered a temporary decline. Today experts hold responsible the explosion of rock and roll. Then, Patsy just knew that it was difficult to get bookings. She didn't fully feel the effects until the fall, and then she was busy at home with a new baby. Julie, Patsy and Charlie's first child, was born in August 1958.

It was almost as if the event had been planned in accordance with her career. Four recording sessions were held the previous year, one of which created the single "Walkin' Dream," which was released at the year's end. In 1958 only one session was scheduled. "Let the Teardrops Fall" and "Never No More" were the results of this effort. None of the records created much of a sensation. It wasn't due to lack of exposure. Patsy continued to work throughout her pregnancy.

Arthur Godfrey and His Friends and the *Ozark Jubilee* were just a couple of her television appearances. Then, there were dates in Nashville, Texas, Minnesota, and even Hawaii. By the time Patsy got to Oahu she was homesick and her ten days in paradise was anything but idyllic. A rare tropical storm that quickly dumped ten inches of rain on the island didn't help her mood, nor did the problems she had getting mail delivered from home. Already on the road for more than a week when the tour began, she didn't expect to be home again for another month. When the trip finally ended she took a much needed rest.

Throughout the year Patsy punctuated spells of working with days of rest, though it's debatable how much rest she actually got at home with all of the cleaning, cooking, and laundry that had to be done. Even before Julie's arrival she seemed more concerned with domestic chores. Though the housework increased after the baby's birth, she seemed in her element. In the letters written to Treva in 1958 Patsy seems content.

She finds herself giving Treva advice. Early in the year Treva announced her plans to marry Bruce Steinbicker. Apparently, Treva's mother wanted her to delay the wedding. Patsy could sympathize with Treva's impatience because she too had to wait to marry, but she could also empathize with Treva's mother. She understood that it was difficult to let go of a child. Finally, her advice to Treva was that if she knew she wouldn't mind washing and ironing and raising babies for him then she should marry him. This statement, perhaps more than any other, reveals just how traditional Patsy was.

Nonetheless, she was in an untraditional role. As much as she enjoyed being a housewife and mother, she adored singing. She loved being on stage and living the life of an entertainer. Unfortunately, when she was ready to go back to work after Julie's birth there was a shortage of show dates. A tour with the Miller Brothers was canceled, and there was little in the way of promotion. She didn't even have a new record to get excited about. Toward the end of the year Decca finally released her 1956 recording of "Dear God." Patsy was optimistic that it would sell, but it was obvious that Decca didn't expect much of a return from it. If the record company had thought it would be a hit, they wouldn't have held it for a year and a half.

As the year ended, Patsy said to Treva, "I sure could stand some work." Once again, the bills were mounting. She was spending more time on local television than on national programs and it must have seemed to her that her career was taking a downward turn. Like the dip in country music sales, this trend was only temporary.

Fayetteville
Jan 26/5?

Dear Irva!

Sorry to be soo
long at writing. I've
been feeling so Bad lately
I'm never feling good any
more. I hate to think I'll
have to be sick like this
far the next eight months.
I'm going to work up till
May, then I'm going to stop
I'll go back to the Godfrey
Show, in April. By the first
of May, I'll be so Big I'll
have to stop working.
    How are you & all the
folks? Tell them all hello

205

\#.

for me, and tell Bruce I'm
glad to hear of that he liked
the little gift. And I wish
you both, the best of luck +
happiness, always. I hope you
are as happy as I + Charlie.
I'm sending you another
money order in a week or two
And I'll try to pay up the
whole thing after this trip to
Minn.
Well I must close + get ready
for bed.
Write soon and send those
post cards, I'll take care
of them.
Take care and be good
Love, Patsy.

Jan 26/ 58

Dear Treva:

Sorry to be so long at writing. I've been feeling so bad lately I'm never feeling good any more. I hate to think I'll have to be sick like this for the next eight months. I'm going to work up till May, then I'm going to stop. I'll go back to the Godfrey Show, in April. By the first of May, I'll be so big I'll have to stop working.

How are you and all the folks? Tell them all hello for me and tell Bruce I'm glad to hear that he liked the little gift. And I wish you both, the best of luck and happiness always. I hope you are as happy as I and Charlie.

I'm sending you another money order in a week or two. And I'll try to pay up the whole thing after this trip to Minn.

Well I must close and get ready for bed.

Write soon and send those post cards. I'll take care of them.

Take care and be good.

Love, Patsy.

Fayetteville
Jan 26/58

Dear Members

I hope all of all you will forgive me for not writing to all of you befor now, But, when you live on the road as much as I do, you welcome a little time at home and I have a lot to do when I do get home.

I guess by now all of you have heard my new record called "Walkin Dream and b/f "Stop The World". The Decca people said it is selling very very well,

II.

I just hope it hits some charts.

I sang both of them while I was visiting with Mr. Godfrey for two weeks last month. We sure had fun, because he always tries to pull some thing on me and I always come out with the dumbest ans.

Another nice thing he did was show my fan awards which I recieved from Cash Box, Bill Board, Juke Box, and Jamboree magazine.

And another thrilling thing that happened over the holidays was Treva & her

III

her mother & Bruce came
to see me. We had a
real ole pow-wow. She
saw my little Cha-
wa-wa dog I got for
Christmas. (my hubby gave
him to me.) Now he's like
one of the family. Ha.

Well, my next show date
is Roanoke, Va., then the Jim
Reeves Show in Nashville then
The Ozark Jubilee on the 15th of Feb.
then the Phillip Morris Show in
Texas. and four days in the
Flame Club in Minn. Minn.
I hope then to come home
for a couple of weeks.
In April, I'll go back to

PATSY CLINE

IV

us, on the Godfrey Show
again.

I hope this finds all
well and good fortune in
1955.

Thanks loads for the
beautiful Christmas gift. It
was very pretty and thanks
for all the nice cards.

I know we artist would-
dnt be artist if it wasnt
for wonderful friends like
all of you.

Thanks again and
I'll sign off saying, be
good and God keep you.
        Your Friend
        Patsy Cline

211

Fayetteville
Jan 26/58

Dear Members

I hope all of you will forgive me for not writing to all of you before now, but, when you live on the road as much as I do, you welcome a little time at home and I have a lot to do when I do get home.

I guess by now all of you have heard my new record called "Walkin' Dream" and b/w "Stop The World." The Decca people said it is selling very very well. I just hope it hits some charts.

I sang both of them while I was visiting with Mr. Godfrey for two weeks last month. We sure had fun, because he always tries to pull something on me and I always come out with the dumbest answer.

Another nice thing he did was show my four awards which I received from "Cash Box," "Bill Board," Juke Box, and Jamboree magazine.

And another thrilling thing that happened over the holidays was Treva and her mother and Bruce came to see me. We had a real ole pow-wow. She saw my little Cha-wa-wa dog I got for Christmas (my hubby gave him to me.) Now he's like one of the family. Ha.

Well, my next show date is Roanoke, Va, then the Jim Reeves Show, in Nashville, then The Ozark Jubilee on the 15th of Feb. then the Phillip Morris Show in Texas, and four days in the Flame Club in Minn., Minn. I hope then to come home for a couple of weeks.

In April, I'll go back to be on the Godfrey Show again. I hope this finds all well and good fortune in 1958.

Thanks loads for the beautiful Christmas gift. It was very pretty and thanks for all the nice cards. I know we artists wouldn't be artists, if it wasn't for wonderful friends like all of you. Thanks again and I'll sign off saying, be good and God Keep You.

Your Friend,
Patsy Cline

The four awards were each for Most Promising Female Country Artist of 1957, which she earned from the success of "Walkin' After Midnight."

•

The new songs, "Stop the World (And Let Me Off)" and "Walking Dream," failed to place in the charts.

Nashville Tenn.
Feb 14/58

Dear Trena:

I talked to Charlie on the phone tonight and he said you had wrote & sent a valintem & the cards, which I thank you for very much.

I'm sorry I hasn't written much but I'm been working on the house what time I'm there and it looks like now I wont be home until the 17th of March. Then I'll be home for only 3 weeks then off for 30 days to 8 weeks in Los Vagas, with the Miller Brothers 10 piece western band.

I'm in Nashville where I just finished the Reeves Show, 6 recordings and the Fri. night Frollic. Tomarrow morning I'm coming to Knoxville for the W.N.O.X Radio Show and then home for Sun & Monday. Then off to

11.

Minn till the 23rd of Feb. then
to California where I'll spend 2 days
with Mr. + Mrs. McCall, then on the 26th
I'll leave for Honolulu Hawaiian
for 10 days all the trip paid for,
and Charlie is coming over if he can
get five or 6 days off. The army
will not charge him to get an army
hop on a plane over there, I sure
hope he gets to come, Then I'll come
home for 3 weeks then off to Las Vagas
from 30 days to 8 weeks, as I told you
then a week on Godfry, and then I
must stop till after the baby.
Oh! I forgot to send you a card but
my sincere congradulations to you both
and I hope you are as happy as I am.
I'm going to have to close and get some
sleep. We recorded from 3. a.m to midnight last night, and I had to get up
early this morning.
Tell all hello and write soon
I'll try to write you while on trips.
Bye now + thanks again
                                 Love
                                   Patsy

Nashville, Tenn.
Feb. 14 /58

Dear Treva:

I talked to Charlie on the phone tonight and he said you had wrote and sent a valentine and the cards, which I thank you for very much.

I'm sorry I haven't written more but I've been working on the house what time I'm there and it looks like now I won't be home until the 17th of March. Then I'll be home for only 3 weeks then off for 30 days to 8 weeks in Las Vegas, with the Miller Brothers 10 piece western band.

I'm in Nashville where I just finished the Reeves Show, 6 recordings and the Fri. night Frolic. Tomorrow morning I'm coming to Knoxville for the W.N.O.X. Radio Show and then home. Minn. till the 23rd of Feb. then to California where I'll spend 2 days with Mr. and Mrs. McCall, then on the 26th I'll leave far Honolulu Hawaii for 10 days all the trip paid for, and Charlie is coming over if he can get five or 6 days off. The army will not charge him to get an army hop on a plane over there. I sure hope he gets to come. Then I'll come home for 3 weeks then off to Las Vegas from 30 days to 8 weeks, as I told you. Then a week on Godfrey, and then I must stop till after the baby.

Oh! I forgot to send you a card but my sincere congratulations to you both and I hope you are as happy as I am. I'm going to have to close and get some sleep. We recorded from 3 PM to midnight last night, and I had to get up early this morning. Tell all "hello" and write soon. I'll try to write you while on trips.

Bye now and thanks again.

Love
Patsy

On February 13, 1958, Patsy recorded six songs: "Just Out of Reach," "I Can See an Angel," "Come On In (And Make Yourself at Home)," "Let the Teardrops Fall," "Never No More," and "If I Could Only Stay Asleep." This was her only recording session for the year.

•

The Friday Night Frolic on WSM is now called the Friday Night Show of the Grand Ole Opry.

Feb 27/58

A-lo-ha

Dear Treva,

Well I'm some where over the blue Pacific and nothing to see but water + more water. Been in the air 3 hours got 5 more to go befor landing in lovely Hawaii. Crazy man crazy.

How is everyone and the beautifull husband to be?? Ha. Tell all "hello" and I sure wish you were with me or some one to talk to. I havn't seen home since Feb 18th and won't get home befor March 31st. Just as soon as I get back to the U.S. Godfrey wants me 2 weeks. I'm going to get Charlie + Godfry a Hawaiian shirt over here. That will please Godfry no end, and people who know I'm expecting are still bawking. They said I could work in maternity clothes. I believe they would let me have it right on stage if I'd work. But I'm stoping in May. Will write you when I get settled. Tell you Mom + aunt hello. Love, Patsy —

Feb. 27/58

A -lo-ha"

Dear Treva:

Well, I'm somewhere over the blue Pacific and nothing to see but water and more water. Been in the air 3 hours, got 5 more to go before landing in lovely Hawaii. Crazy man crazy.

How is everyone and the beautiful husband to be? Ha. Tell all "hello" and I sure wish you were with me or someone to talk to. I haven't seen home since Feb. 18th and won't get home before March 31st. Just as soon as I get back to the U.S. Godfrey wants me 2 weeks. I'm going to get Charlie and Godfrey a Hawaiian shirt over here. That will please Godfrey no end. And people who know I'm expecting are still booking. They said I could work in maternity clothes. I believe they would let me have it right on stage if I'd work. But I'm stopping in May. I'll write you when I get settled. Tell your Mom and Aunt "hello."

Love Patsy.

March 6/58

Dear Treva:

While the flood waters are going down I thought I'd drop you a few lines. Yes, I said flood waters. Within 24 hours over here they have had 10 inches of rain just pouring down. It rained for 24 hours solid. I'm so sick of it I could scream. The whole town is a mess. The streets and sidewalks are covered and the basement of the biggest hotel here is parking for 300 cars and every one of the cars are covered over the top with water. They are pulling them out today. I'd hate to be one owner without insurance. The sun is breaking out now and I sure hope it stays out. I've never been so home sick, lonesome, tired, disgusted, and worried in all my life. I've been here 8 days and still not one piece of mail from home or Charles. He sent a telegram to say he had wrote, but I still can't understand why I haven't gotten any mail. I've wrote every day to him. The office girl said that people never have any trouble getting their mail here if it comes by air mail and I know he sent it by air. I'm just sick. I've been ready to go home 3 days ago. You stay here a week and then it's the same ole thing and it gets very boring. Oh! It's nice and plenty of sunshine when it shines, but I've seen all I want to see of it.

I'll leave here Mon. morning and do four shows in California, then to the Godfrey Show if he can use me then, for 2 weeks. Then 10 days in Denver and 30 days to 8 weeks in Vegas. Then I'm finished. I'm not doing another thing till after it's all over in Sept. I'm beginning to show now anyway. Can't wear western clothes or tight dresses any more. I'll be so glad when I can stay at home, and live a little. I cut my hair short and got a permanent. It's a lot easier to handle now. I'll send you a pair of shoes like they wear over here. Even the children, men, and all, everywhere and every day. You can wear them this summer. I like them a lot.

Well, I'll close and get a few more letters off and you write soon. The army, navy, and air force and marines are sure over here and do they ever hate this place. Sure are a lot from Tenn., Kentucky, Va . and W. Va. They like "Stop The World" over here better than I like to do it. Been having real good crowds. Sometimes 6 or 8 thousand.

Tell all "hello" and I'll write as soon as I can get a place to stop long enough to set down. So long for now.

Love,
Patsy.

Patsy Cline in her famous purple and white dress.
From Treva's personal scrapbook, courtesy of Bruce Steinbicker.

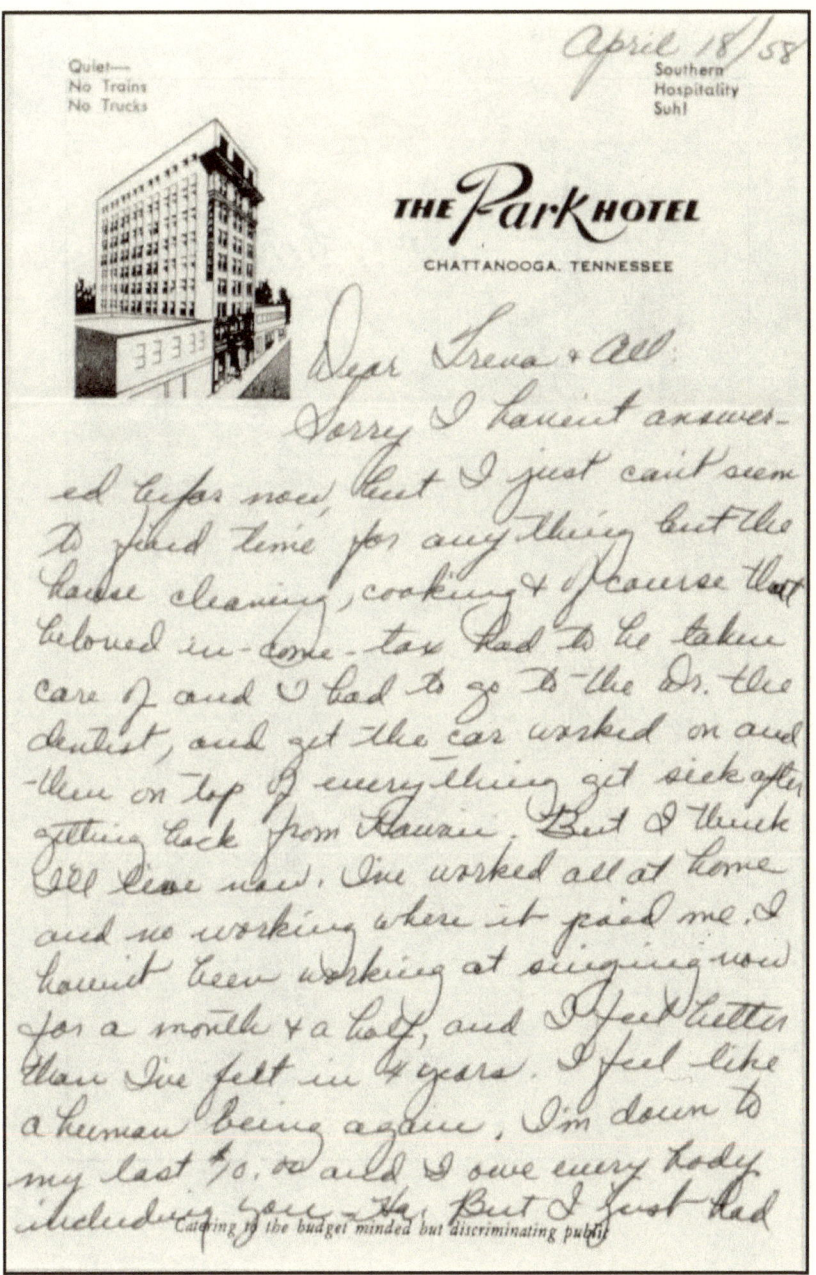

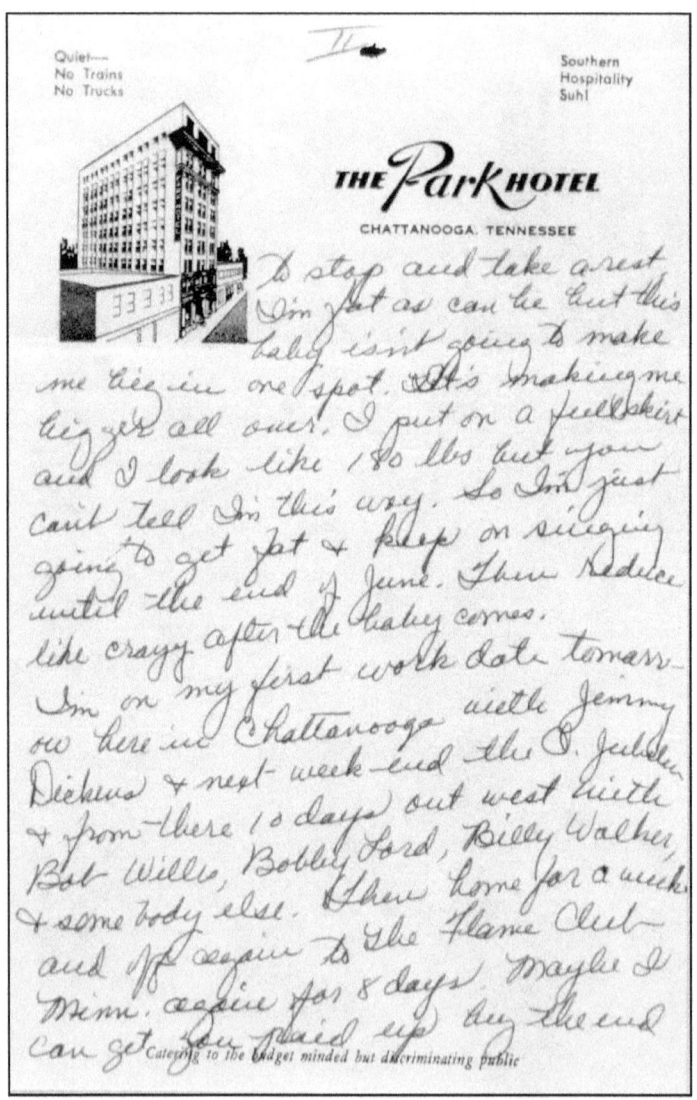

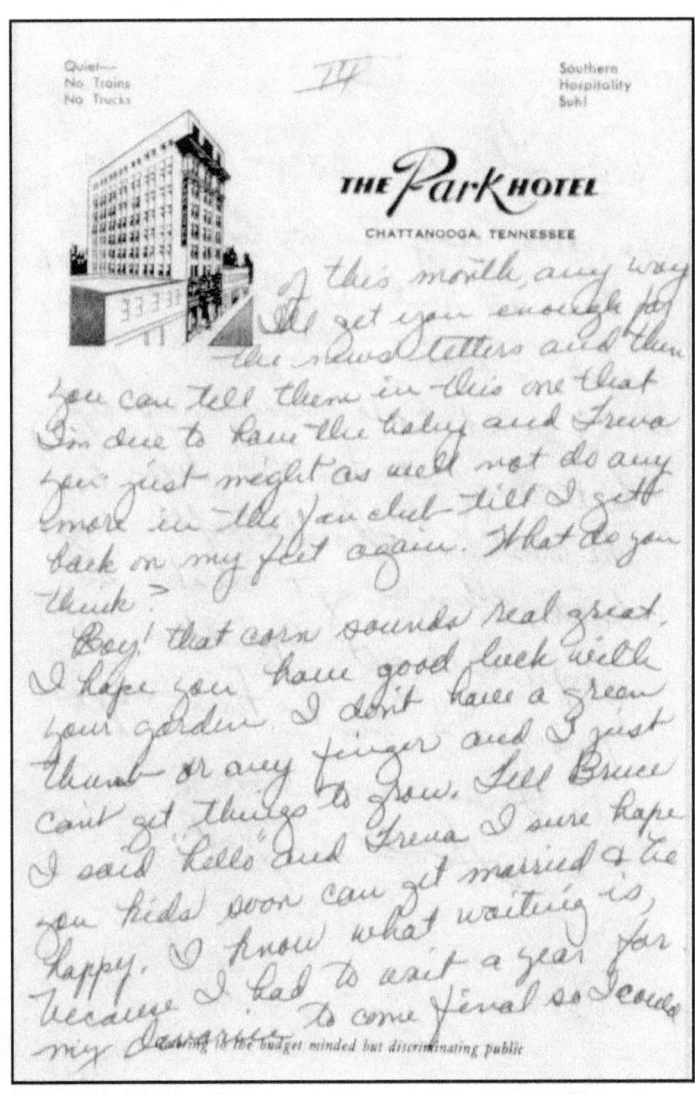

IV -

some shoes or boots on this youngin.
I'm not the only one with the stork
on the way. "Martha Carson" just had
an 8 lb baby boy, "June Carter" is expecting, "Ferlin Huskey's wife "Betty" is,
& "Goldie Hill" also, and even "Rose Mary
Clooney" & "Carmel Quinn" on the Godfrey Show.
   So "Jean Shepard, & Wonda Jackson
& Jeane Roman, it's up to you gals
to keep us women going in this
music field.
   Well, I guess I'd better sign off
and get ready for my show here
in Chattonooga tonite with "Jimmy
Dickens" & George Morgan". Chattonooga
is where I am right now.
   Don't forget our gal Irena, write
to her or she will keep you posted
while Bruce. Keeps spining good
country music. God Be with you all
   your Friend Patsy
                            Cline

April 18 /58

Dear Treva and All:

Sorry I haven't answered before now but I just can't seem to find time for anything but the house cleaning, cooking and of course that beloved in-come-tax had to be taken care of and I had to go to the Dr. the dentist, and get the car worked on and then on top of everything got sick after getting back from Hawaii. But I think I'll live now. I've worked all at home and no working where it paid me. I haven't been working at singing now for a month and a half, and I feel better than I've felt in 4 years. I feel like a human being again. I'm down to my last $10.00 and I owe everybody including you. Ha. But I just had to stop and take a rest. I'm fat as can be but this baby isn't going to make me big in one spot. It's making me bigger all over. I put on a full skirt and I look like 180 lbs but you can't tell I'm this way. So I'm just going to get fat and keep on singing until the end of June. Then reduce like crazy after the baby comes.

I'm on my first work date tomorrow here in Chattanooga with Jimmy Dickens and next weekend the 0. Jubilee and from there 10 days out west with Bob Wills, Bobby Lord, Billy Walker, and somebody else. Then home for a week and off again to the Flame Club in Minn. again for 8 days.

Maybe I can get you paid up by the end of this month, any way I'll get you enough for the newsletters and then you can tell them in this one that I'm due to have the baby and Treva you just might as well not do any more in the fan club till I get back on my feet again. What do you think?

Boy! that corn sounds really great. I hope you have good luck with your garden. I don't have a green thumb or any finger and I just can't get things to grow. Tell Bruce I said "hello" and Treva I sure hope you kids soon can get married and be happy. I know what waiting is, because I had to wait a year for my divorce to come final so I could marry this jug head. But I hope you are as happy as we are really soon. I know and understand why your Mother objects. You are all she has and you are her baby, but then too, all these chickens have to find out about life their own way no matter how much we love them or try to talk and teach them. You have to have a life of your own sooner or later and she should thank God she will be here on earth to help you with all your heartaches and troubles even tho you are a wife. Don't get mad at her, she's just Mom and all Moms are like that, and it's because she don't want to lose you so soon in life. But if Bruce is the one and you know nothing on earth can keep you apart and that you'll never mind washing and ironing, raising babies for him, I'd say then, don't give up and marry him while this ole world is still here.

I'm not trying to be a preacher, but I'm writing a book it looks like. By the way. I've got 2000 pictures being made now and I'll send you some before long. Well I'm glad you liked the shoes. Tell your Mom and Aunt Lizzy I said "hello" and you all don't get too much Spring fever.

Got to get a little sleep and I'll finish the Fan Club letter in the morning. Write soon and be good. Your Friend Always,

Love

Patsy

P.S. On my income tax total of plane fares, for 57 it was $4500.00, just plane tickets. I could own one of them things.

PS. The Dr. says this young'in is due Aug 30th but I think he's all wet. I still say the first 2 weeks of Sept.

I would have been on Godfrey show but they cut his T.V. time and he was in Florida after I got back. Then I got sick so maybe I'll get up there in May. He don't know yet about my condition. Good night.

In 1998 Jimmy Dickens celebrated fifty years of performing on the Grand Ole Opry.

•

Round trip plane fare in 1957 was around $150 from Nashville to Los Angeles.

Howdy Again Everyone:

Been a long time between letters here but I'll try to fill you in on why I haven't been keeping in touch. Since the new year started I've been busy with the Godfrey Show, the Flame Club in Minn., California, Chicago with the Phillip Morris Show, the Jim Reeves Show, recording sessions and a 2 week trip with Ferlin Husky, Jerry Reed and Faron Young to beautiful Hawaii. Got a good sun tan and just had a big time seeing all the service men. They said to tell you all, "Hello" and they sure do wish they could be home. When I got back from Hawaii, I did a Phillip show again and got sick while in Chicago. Well when the Dr. came, he said I had to take a long rest, so for 1½ mons. now I've been busy being a house wife and spring cleaning and getting the nursery in shape for our new addition.

Yes, I'm going to have my first baby the first of Sept. I knew it long before I went to Hawaii, but I thought I could keep on singing awhile, but I'll stop in June until the little one gets here. We hope for a boy, but we'll be glad to take Pot luck. Ha.

The next time you see me, you won't know me I'm so fat.

This April 26th I'll see you on the Country Music Jubilee and then I'll be on a 10 day tour with "Bob Wills." Then to the Flame Club again in Minn. with "Texas Bill Strength."

Enough about me, how are all the wonderful fans and friends of mine? I'll bet every one of you have spring fever. Don't work too hard at those flower gardens, and that house cleaning will have to be done in two weeks time all over again. I sure hope you all will go see the movie called "Country Music Holiday" with Ferlin, Faron, June Carter, the Ladell Sisters and Rod Brassfield. It's a scream.

I've got a new record coming out in a week or

two called "Let The Tear-Drops Fall" and b/w "Just Out of Reach." Yes, "Just Out Of Reach" was recorded by Faron Young some time ago and I've recut it with the Anita Kerrs. So if you like it, we'll sure appreciate you taking a copy home so I can put some shoes or boots on this youngin. I'm not the only one with the stork on the way. "Martha Carson" just had an 8 lb baby boy, "June Carter" is expecting, Ferlin Husky's wife "Betty" is, and "Goldie Hill" also, and even "Rosemary Clooney" and "Carmel Quinn" on the Godfrey Show.

So Jean Shepard, and Wanda Jackson and Mimi Roman, it's up to you gals to keep us women going in the music field. Well, I guess I'd better sign off and get ready for my show here in Chattanooga tonite with "Jimmy Dickens" and "George Morgan." (Chattanooga is where I am right now.) Don't forget our gal Treva, write to her and she will keep you posted while Bruce keeps spinning *good country music.*

God Be With You All.

Your Friend,
Patsy Cline

Texas Bill Strength, who was also a singer and disc jockey, booked Patsy to perform at the Flame Club, a popular Minnesota nightclub, several times.

•

The late George Morgan is better known today as the father of star Lorrie Morgan.

This is one of the few photos taken of Patsy as a riding cowgirl.
From Treva's personal scrapbook, courtesy Bruce Steinbicker.

Fayetteville
June 13/58

Dear Irene:

I suppose you are having a very busy time about now getting things in shape for the big doing s, and I'm sure happy for you & Bruce. I got your letter & the clipping out of the paper. Sure wish you could send me a picture of the wedding. It was a nice write up & a good picture –

Well, I guess you will have to forget all about the ~~fan~~ ~~album~~ club till after Oct Irene, because I've got $1050. & thats got

to be paid befor the end
of the month or I'll lose
every-thing, so I don't have
any money for stamps to
mail the journals if I
could hace them wrote
up. So if you can, we
will start all over & I'll pay
up as soon as I get back
to work. The baby sure does
make me feel bad any more.
It kicks like crazy all the
time and it so hot in this
place, you can fry.
Sylvia, my sister is here
with me now for the sum-
mer to help me out, and I
sure am glad.
Mom is going to sell the

brick house & move to Florida. She can get $12000.00 out of the big house & buy one in Florida for $8500.00. One that has the landscaping, big picture windows, car port, colored bath room, glass sliding doors to the patio, & 5 rooms, & hardwood floors & tile in the bath & kitchen. Can you think of that all for $8500.00. They only ask $2000. down & $66.00 a month. I told Charlie I would like to live down there after he gets out, but he says he wants to go to Nashville. So I don't know yet. But we have got to go some place where

I can work and he can get a good job also.

We have the dog back from my aunts in Florida now, and he's about 1 size bigger than he was, but still as full of life as always. Spoiled so bad I can't hardly live with them

Well, I guess I'd better close & get a little rest. Got to go to the Dr. tomorrow or the next day so, he can prog around & hurt some more! I hate to go to the Dr.

Write soon & I hope you & Bruce are as happy as Charlie & I. Tell your Mom & Aunt "hello."

Love always, Patsy.

Fayetteville
June 15/58

Dear Treva:

I suppose you are having a very busy time about now getting things in shape for the big doings, and I'm sure happy for you and Bruce. I got your letter and the clipping out of the paper. Sure wish you could send me a picture of the wedding. It was a nice write up and a good picture.

Well, I guess you will have to forget all about the fan club till after Oct. Treva, because I've got $1050 .00 that's got to be paid before the end of the month or I'll lose everything, so I don't have any money for stamps to mail the journals if I could have them wrote up. So if you can, we will start all over and I'll pay up as soon as I get back to work. The baby sure does make me feel bad any more. It kicks like crazy all the time and it's so hot in this place, you can fry. Sylvia, my sister is here with me now for the summer to help me out, and I sure am glad.

Mom is going to sell the brick house and move to Florida. She can get $12000.00 out of the big house and buy one in Florida for $8500.00. One that has the landscaping, big picture windows, car port, colored bath room, glass sliding doors to the patio and 5 rooms, and hardwood floors and tile in bath and kitchen. Can you think of that all for $8500.00? They only ask $2000 down and $66.00 a month. I told Charlie I would like to live down there after he gets out, but he says he wants to go to Nashville. So I don't know yet. But we have got to go some place where I can work and he can get a good job also.

We have the dog back from my aunts in Florida now, and he's about 1 size bigger than he was, but still as full of life as always. Spoiled so bad I can't hardly live with them. Well, I guess I'd better close and get a little rest. Got to go to the Dr. tomorrow or the next day so he can prod around and hurt some more. I hate to go to the Dr.

Write soon and I hope you and Bruce are as happy as Charlie and I. Tell your Mom and Aunt "hello."

Love always, Patsy

Patsy Cline Weds Sunday

The marriage of Mrs. Virginia Hensley Cline, of Winchester, Va. and Pvt. Charles Allen Dick, also of Winchester, occured Sunday afternoon at the home of the bride's mother, 720 South Kent street, Winchester.

The double ring ceremony was performed by Rev. S. J. Goode of Winchester before a background of white gladioli, white carnations and ferns.

Given in marriage by her brother, Sam L. Hensley, Jr., the bride wore a two piece light blue knit dress with white hat, gloves, blue shoes, and a corsage of white rosebuds.

Miss Sylvia Mae Hensley, sister of the bride, was maid of honor and Miss Patsy Lillis was bridesmaid.

Miss Nancy Conner of Kernstown, Va., was flower girl.

William L. Dick was best man for his brother.

A reception was held Sunday evening at 8 o'clock at Mountainside Inn on Route 50, West of Winchester.

Mrs. Dick, known professionally as Patsy Cline, is a recording and television artist and is under contract to Decca Records. She plans to continue her career and the first of October she will go on a Southern tour with Porter Wagner, Johnny Cash and Bobby Helms.

Pvt. Dick, son of Mrs. I. E. Dick, and the late Mr. Dick, is serving with the U. S. Army stationed at Fort Bragg, N. C.

Treva and Bruce married on June 20, 1958. They chose this date because both of their parents had married on this day exactly twenty-two years before.

•

Patsy's mother decided not to move to Florida.

Wenchester, Va
Aug 18/58

Dear Treva,

Thought I'd get a few lines
off to you before work time so I
could let you know the news.
Yes! I said work. The man
from the Dixie Pig down in Wash.
called and said he would like
to have me 4 days if I could
work. So I said, "if you can stand
it I can." Ha. So I started last
Fri. the 15th and tonight is my
last night, and no one still can
tell there is any thing wrong with
me unless I tell them. They said
"you have gained a little weight
havint you?", but they don't think
that it's time for me to go to the
hospital. Yes! This coming

241

Seen the 25th I go to the hospital and the Dr. is going to give me a shot and start me Monday morning because I'm ready and getting along good and it's no use waiting till the 30th because I'm just fooling time & I'd be gaining more weight. So I'm ready and glad that I can get it over with. I'm at Mom's and Charlie is taking 10 days leave starting Sat. so he will be there to take me to the hospital. So Irma, we will soon know what it is. I'm betting Charley it's a girl but he says (and wont give up) that it's a boy. I've been carrying it awhfull high tho. Anyway I dont care what it is just so it gets here and is healthy. It sure does know how to kick. Never lets up.

I looked for you last week end and this past week end, but didn't hear or see you. I hope everything is O.K. and all the family is fine. Tell your Mom Hubby & Aunt "Lillo" for me.

My new record is "Record of the Week" here in Va, N.C. & Wash. They like "Never No More" better than "I Can See An Angel." I don't like either one of them. But "Never No-more" has the same beat that Walkin did. I'm keeping my fingers crossed.

Well, I'll close. Got to write to Susie Arden & tell her the news, and two or three others. So write and write to me in the hospital. I'll be there 5 days from 24th to 28th. Just write

to the "Winchester Memorial Hosp.
Winchester, Va". to Patsy Cline Dick
O.B. floor. I'll get it fine and as
soon as I know I'll let you know
too. Be good and take
care of yourself. Come to see
me when you can.
Love always
Patsy Cline.

P.S. Ferlin Husky C.B.S. time
is taking Godfrey till Fall and Maxine
not show, Jim & Bonnie Brown are quitting
the busness all together. Jim is
going in with his dad & Maxine
is going home, take care of her baby.
I don't know what Bonnie
will do. Just a little news.

Winchester, Va.
Aug. 18 / 58

Dear Treva:

Thought I'd get a few lines off to you before work time so I could let you know the news.

Yes! I said work. The man from the Dixie Pig down in Wash. called and said he would like to have me 4 days if I could work. So I said, "if you can stand it I can." Ha. So I started last Fri. the 15th and tonight is my last night, and no one still can tell there is anything wrong with me unless I tell them. They said "You have gained a little weight haven't you?", but they don't think that it's time for me to go to the hospital. Yes! This coming Sun. the 25th I go to the hospital and the Dr. is going to give me a shot and start me Monday morning because I'm ready and getting along good and it's no use waiting till the 30th because I'm just fooling time and I'd be gaining more weight. So I'm ready and glad that I can get it over with. I'm at Mom's and Charlie is taking 10 days leave starting Sat. so he will be there to take me to the hospital. So Treva, we will soon know what it is. I'm betting Charlie it's a girl, but he says (and won't give up) that it's a boy. I've been carrying it awful high tho. Anyway I don't care what it is just so it gets here and is healthy. It sure does know how to kick. Never lets up.

I looked for you last weekend and this past weekend, but didn't hear or see you. I hope everything is O.K. and all the family is fine. Tell your Mom, Hubby and Aunt "hello" for me.

My new record is "Record of The Week" here in Va., N.C. and Wash. They like "Never No More" better than " I Can See An Angel. " I don't like either one of them. But "Never No More" has the same beat that Walkin did. I'm keeping my fingers crossed. Well, I'll close. Got to write to Suzie Arden and tell her the news, and two or three others. So write and write to me in the hospital. I'll be there 5 days from 24th to 28th. Just write to the " Winchester Memorial Hosp. Winchester, Va." To Patsy Cline Dick 0.B.

floor. I'll get it fine and as soon as I know I'll let you know. Ha. Be good and take care of yourself. Come to see me when you can.

Love Always,
Patsy Cline.

PS. Ferlin Husky is taking Godfrey C.B.S. <u>time</u> not show, till fall and Maxine Jim and Bonnie Brown are quitting the business all together. Jim is going in with his dad and Maxine is going home, take care of her boy. I don't know what Bonnie will do. Just a little news.

Neither Patsy nor record buyers liked the recordings "Never No More" and "I Can See an Angel", which did not place on the charts. Patsy would not have a hit song again until "I Fall to Pieces" in 1961.

Winchester, Va
Aug 27/58

Dear Treva:

Thought I'd drop you a few lines while laying here in this ole hospital waiting for Julie to come in to be fed. This place is for the birds. I'm in a simi-private and the other bed was emptied yesterday and no one is in here with me. The visiting hours are only 2 hrs. a day from 3 to 4 & 7 to 8. Everybody I think has sent cards, called and every night a big bunch comes to see us.

My little Julie is sure popular. Of course everyone is full of curiosity to see

what P. Clines baby looks like.
But even if I do say so,
she is pretty. We are soo
proud of her, we are almost
ready to pop. She weighed
6 lbs 3 ozs, 19½ in. long and has
blue black eyes + dark brown
hair. Her eyes will turn to
brown I'm sure because both
of us have brown. Treva, I
don't think I'll ever want to
go through that again, but
I'm sure glad I did this
time and I feel like a real
woman now. Those labor
hours are living hell. I came
in the hospital (in no pain)
at 10 P.m. to bed at 10:30 P.m.
At 11 P.m. the Dr. broke my
water + ½ hr. later I was have
my pains 6 mins apart.

III.

When they gave me a shot I would come & go then and from then on out I was a screaming mess until she was born at 3:25 A.M. I remember her head was coming through when they gave me ither. I got 3 breaths full of ither and went out like a light. I didn't get to see her till Monday morning at 8 or 9: A.M. But Charlie & Mom saw her at 4:15 A.M. I get to feed her 3 times a day.

Every time I get her with me she goes to sleep, but the baby D. said she was in the best of health So thats all that matters.

Well how is every one & every thing with all of

IV

you? Tell all the folks
"hello" for us and tell
them we will be writing
for you all to come see
us when ever possible.
The paper came today and
took our pictures, so when
I get them I'll send you one
of them.
I worked the Dixie Pig 4 days
Wash. the week. and you were
by the house. I told them
at the "Pig" if they could stand
it I could & had standing
room only the four days I was
there. So the first of Oct
I'll be back at the job.
Well I'll close & you write
soon and tell Bruce "hello"
and he better catch up with us.
Ha Ha. Just kidding.

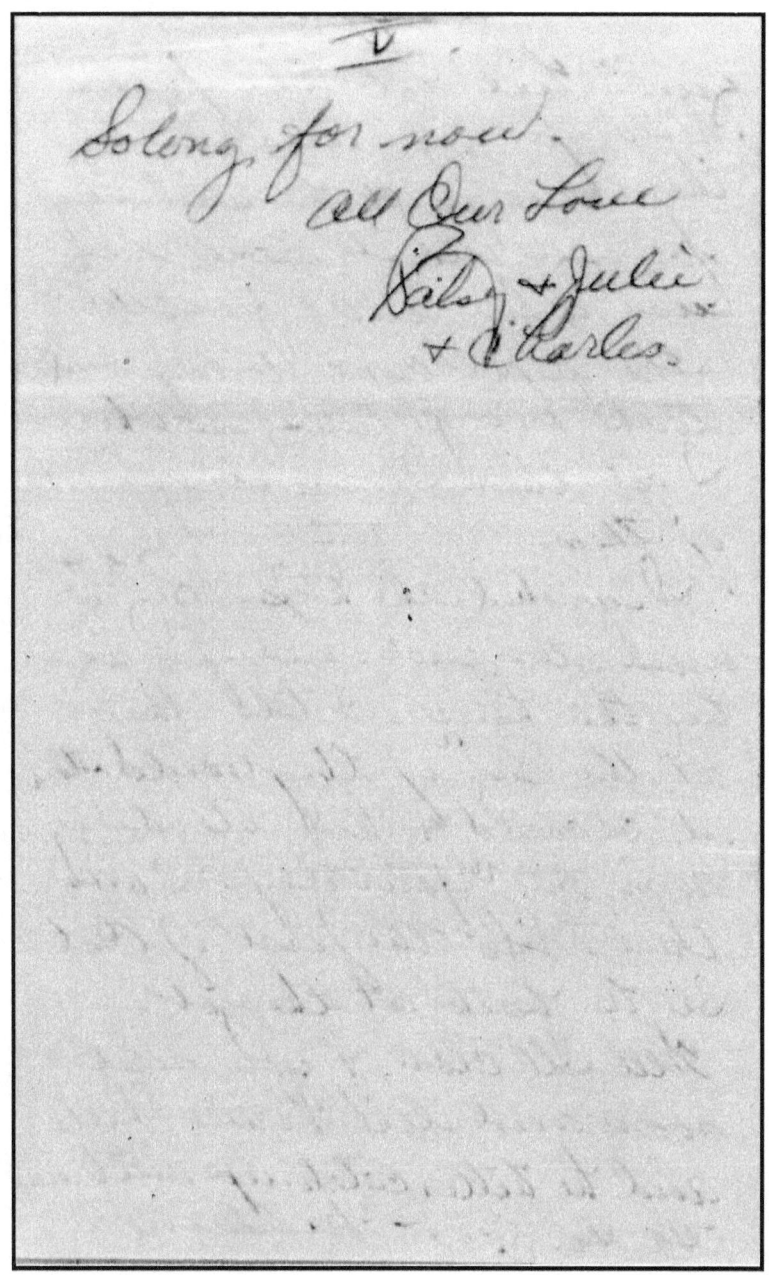

Winchester, Va.
Aug 27/58

Dear Treva:

Thought I'd drop you a few lines while laying here in this ole hospital waiting for Julie to come in to be fed. This place is for the birds. I'm in a semi-private and the other bed was emptied yesterday and no one is in here with me. The visiting hours are only 2 hrs. a day from 3 to 4 and 7 to 8. Everybody I think has sent cards, called, and every night a big bunch comes to see us.

My little Julie is sure popular. Of course everyone is full of curiosity to see what P. Cline's baby looks like. But even if I do say so, she is pretty. We are soo proud of her, we are almost ready to pop. She weighed 6 lbs. 3 ozs, 19½ in. long and has blue black eyes and dark brown hair. Her eyes will turn to brown I'm sure because both of us have brown. Treva, I don't think I'll ever want to go through that again, but I'm sure glad I did this time and I feel like a real woman now. Those labor hours are living hell. I came in the hospital (in no pain) at 10:P.M. to bed at 10:30 P.M. At 11:P,M. the Dr. broke my water and ½ hr. later I was having pains 6 mins. apart. When they gave me a shot I would come and go then and from then on out I was a screaming mess until she was born at 3:25 A.M. I remember her head was coming through when they gave me ether. I got 3 breaths full of ether and went out like a light. I didn't get to see her till Monday morning at 8 or 9:AM. but Charlie and Mom saw her at 4:15 AM. I get to feed her 3 times a day.

Every time I get her with me she goes to sleep, but the baby Dr. said she was in the best of health. So that's all that matters.

Well how is everyone and everything with all of you? Tell all the folks "hello" for us and tell them we will be waiting for you all to come see us whenever possible.

The paper came today and took our pictures, so when I get them I'll send you one of them.

I worked the Dixie Pig 4 days in Wash. the weekend you were by the *house. I told them at the Pig "if they could stand it I could" and had standing room only the four days I was there. So the first of Oct. I'll be back at the job.*

Well I'll close and you write soon and tell Bruce "hello" and he better catch up with us. Ha Ha. Just kidding.

So long for now.

> *All Our Love*
> *Patsy and Julie*
> *and Charles*

Julie's full name was Julia Simadore Dick. Her middle name was taken from the Bible. Simadore was Delilah's sister.

•

Patsy and Charlie did have another child. Their son, Randy, was born on January 22, 1961.

I'll miss the conven-
tion, darn it. on tour. Winchester, Va
Oct 19/58

Dear Treva:

I soppose you do think
I'm dead but I've just got so
much to do with a little one
around. But we are all fine,
I just got back from a week
with friends in N.C. with Charlie
The Raley & I were down. I'm not
working until Nov. 9th 30 day
tour with the Miller Brothers,
Starts in Texas. No body is
working & I can't get hold of
Godfrey. He sent a huage spray
of flowers. Taron sent a bentine
set. Everyone's been wonderful
and thanks so very very much
for the bottle holder. She really
needed it & uses it all the time.
Well Julie now is 18 lbs, + has already had pictures made but I
got to get them yet, I'll write
more later. Love to Patsy. +
all. Julie.

Winchester, Va.
Oct. 19/58

Dear Treva:

Suppose you do think I'm dead but I've just got so much with a little one around. But we are all fine. I just got back from a week with friends in N.C. with Charlie. The baby and I were down. I' m not working until Nov. 9th 30 day tour with the Miller Brothers. Starts in Texas. Nobody is working and I can't get hold of Godfrey. He sent a huge spray of flowers. Faron sent a buntin set. Everyone's been wonderful, and thanks so very very much for the bottle holder. She really needed it and uses it all the time.

Well Julie now is 10 lbs. and has already had pictures made but I got to get them yet. I'll write more later.

Love to all.
Patsy and Julie.
P.S. I like your stationery gal. I could use some couldn't I? Ha.

The Miller Brothers were an instrumental group founded by a family of brothers named Gibbs. In the 1950s the band recorded and toured with fellow 4 Star artists.

P.S. I like you stationary gal.
I could use some couldn't I? Ha

Winchester, Va.
Oct, 22/58

Dear Treva:

Sorry I took so long to write but I've been in D.C. with Charles a week and am working radio one nite a week & Sat nites with Don Owens in D.C. on T.V. (local). It sure doesn't pay any thing but at least I'm still befor the public around here. I'm starting a (at least) 30 day tour Nov 9th in Texas with the Miller Bros. I'll be back at the Flame in Minn. over the D.J. conven. darn it. I wanted to go so bad because I hear H. Thompson is to be there for the Dance in the ball room.

II,

Anyway, no one else will work during the conven. so Im hard up & stuck with it. Are you & Bruce going? Charlie wanted to go see Hank J. so bad as well as to see everyone. We are all fine & hope you are the same. Tell all hello for me. Julie now weighs 10 lbs stripped & is 21½ in long. Two in. more than she was at birth, & is spoiled terrible. All the friends of mine are doing it for me. She coos & laughs at everyone now. I got the proofs of her pictures so Ill get them made & send you a small one. Im playing Norfolk, Va Oct 31. at with the "Texas Wild cats." How about that? They are not

I4,

with Connie B. Gay now because George Hamilton went off
you know + Connie doesn't
have them any work so they are
on their own now.
If I can make $3100.00 + door $2400.00 on this
tour the 9+9 Treva, maybe
I can send you a $100.00 to
get the club going again, but
I've got $1600.00 to pay out
of that here for bills and
my transportation for 30 days
out of that will run about $500.
but if I can swing it, I'll
sure try to get it going again
because I've got a 100 new
members I know of ready to
join as soon as I'm back at
it again.
"How is my new record do-
ing there?" "If I Could See The
World". It's sold out here 3 times

IV

and is getting a lot of plays
around the house, but I doubt
if it will do any chart making. Tell Bruce I thank
him loads for spining them.
Well I've got to get to bed
& wash Julies clothes tomorrow,
I have to wash twice a wk now.
Write soon and come see
us & I hope you get your house
before long. I only wish I could
get one. Things are so rough
here & Mom & my brother don't
like Charlie & I've been so upset lately I couldn't write to
any one. Two families in one
house just wont work, and I
cant keep them anymore. That
is what it comes down to; but
that's life I guess. You get plenty,
you want more always. Oh Well
write soon & be good. Patsy &
Love to all.   Julie.

Winchester, Va.
Oct. 22/58

Dear Treva:

Sorry I took so long to write but I've been in N.C. with Charles a week and am working radio one nite a week and Sat nites with Don Owens in D.C. on T.V. (local). It sure doesn't pay anything but at least I'm still before the public around here. I'm starting a (at last) 30 day tour Nov 9th in Texas with the Miller Bros. I'll be back at the Flame in Minn. over the DJ conven. darn it. I wanted to go so bad because I hear H. Thompson is to be there for the dance in the ball room. Anyway, no one else will work during the convent. So I'm hard up and stuck with it.

Are you and Bruce going? Charlie wanted to go see Hank T. so bad as well as to see everyone. We are all fine and hope you are the same. Tell all "hello" for me.

Julie now weighs 10 lb. stripped and is 21½ in long. Two in. more than she was at birth, and is spoiled terrible. All the friends of mine are doing it for me. She coos and laughs at everyone now. I got the proofs of her pictures, so I'll get them made and send you a small one. I'm playing Norfolk, Va. Oct. 31st with the "Texas Wildcats." How about that? They are not with Connie B. Gay now because George Hamilton went off you know and Connie doesn't have them any work so they are on their own now.

If I can make $3100.00 and clear $2400.00 on this tour (the 9th) Treva, maybe I can send you a $100.00 to get the club going again, but I've got $1600.00 to pay out of that here for bills and my transportation for 30 days out of that will run about $500, but if I can swing it, I'll sure try get it going again because I've got a 100 new members I know of ready to join as soon as I'm back at it again.

How is my new record doing there? "If I Could See The World." It's sold out here 3 times and is getting a lot of plays around in here, but I doubt if it will do any chart making. Tell Bruce I thank him loads for spinning them.

Well I've got to get to bed and wash Julie's clothes tomorrow. I have to wash twice a week now.

Write soon and come see us and I hope you get your house before long. I only wish I could get one. Things are so tough here and Mom and my brother don't like Charlie and I've been so upset lately I couldn't write to anyone. Two families in one house just won't work, and I can't keep them anymore. That is what it comes down to, but that's life I guess. You get plenty, you want more always. Oh well, write soon and be good.

Love to all
Patsy and
Julie.

PS. Charlie has 85 days to go in army.

Hank Thompson was a successful bandleader, singer, and writer. He was elected to the Country Music Hall of Fame in 1989.

•

Don Owens was a country music disc jockey and television host in Washington, D.C. He would later create one of the first bluegrass festivals in the country.

P.S. Charlie has 85 days to go in army.

Winchester, Va
Dec 8/58

Dear Treva & Bruce:

Sorry to be so late writing but I had five days in Minn then the car went bad, then (& now) Julie is sick with cold & infected ears & throat. No work and none in sight. Didn't get to go to the convention either. They have canceled 60 days work on me since Aug 29th. The thirty days I told you about was canceled also except for the 5 days in Minn over the days of the convention of course. They said Jimmy Dean came into from the air port by police escort & had all Columbia artist to meet & greet him in lobby of the hotel. Some deal Huh? Said Ferlin Husky has put back on his western wear & I'm glad to hear it. So am I. Well, finally "Dear God" has been

II.

released. I finally got them to get it out of Decca. Don't know if you have heard of this song or not. It's been recorded for over a 10 yr &. and only given out to D. J.'s but never for sale, so now it's for sale and has been released. It's my first real release record. I've gotten 2500 letters already around this part of the country for the record. People wanting it and I believe it will sell. I'm getting ready for a session of 2 singles and he wants me to cut an album also but I don't think I want an album on Decca. I've only got till May 59. with McCall Dewey if my recollection is right on my contract. Then either to "Dot" or "R.C.A.".

Well I hope all are well and everything is going good for you. Tell your Mom & Aunt "hello". I sure could stand some work that way for $100. per nite, so see what you can do.

Love Patsy + Julie.

Winchester, Va.
Dec. 8/58

Dear Treva and Bruce:

Sorry to be so late writing but I had five days in Minn. then the car went bad, then (and now) Julie is sick with cold and infected ears and throat. No work and none in sight. Didn't get to go to the convention either. They have canceled 60 days work on me since Aug 29th. The thirty days I told you about was canceled (no money they say) also except for the 5 days in Minn. over the days of the convention of course.

They said Jimmy Dean came in from the airport by police escort and had all Columbia artists to meet and greet him in lobby of the hotel. Some deal Huh? Said Ferlin Husky has put back on his western wear and I'm glad to hear it. So am I. Well, finally " Dear God" has been released. I finally got them to get it out of Decca. Don't know if you have heard of this song or not. It's been recorded for over a 1 yr. ½, and only given out to DJs but never for sale, so now it's for sale and has been released. It's my first real religious record. I've gotten 2500 letters already around this part of the country for the record. People wanting it and I believe it will sell. I'm getting ready for a session of 2 singles and he wants me to cut an album also, but I don't think I want an album on Decca. I've only got till May 59 with Decca McCall if my recollection is right on my contract. Then either to "Dot" or "R.C.A."

Well I hope all are well and everything is going good for you. Tell your Mom and Aunt "hello."

I sure could stand some work that way. $100 per nite, so see what you can do.

Love
Patsy and Julie

"Dear God" was recorded in April 1956 but not released until December 1958.

1959

On January 22, 1959, we reach the last letter in this collection.

Perhaps it's fitting that the story ends for us here. With her marriage, Treva is beginning a new chapter in life and it's a turning point for Patsy as well. Although this last letter is brief, it is full of hope and possibility. Enthused by a couple of recording sessions, she proclaims, "I really have something different this time."

Though she doesn't mention it, this was the first of her sessions to be recorded in stereo. No doubt Owen Bradley and the engineers were excited about the introduction of stereo recording. Decca had not yet agreed to actually release their country artists' records in stereo, and playbacks were still in mono. Still, this was cutting-edge technology that would ultimately be important to Patsy's music's longevity.

What excited her most about the sessions were the vocals, and here she was breaking ground too. On the song "Yes, I Understand," she overdubbed the harmonies. Patsy was not the first to try this technique, but it was a trick not often used and it delighted her. An important part of Patsy's new sound was the introduction of the Jordanaires on backing vocals. From this point on, they would appear on all but one of her sessions.

Although the 1959 winter sessions did not produce a hit, they seemed to lay the groundwork for Patsy's future success. Owen Bradley was developing the sound that would bring Patsy to the top of the charts and everlasting fame. If Owen and Patsy had their choice of songs, this might have happened sooner, but for now they were still tied to 4 Star's contract and Bill McCall's control of the song catalogue. That contract would end in 1960.

Patsy was taking charge of her career. In the late summer of 1959 Patsy, Charlie, and Julie moved to Nashville. She wouldn't be a bystander to the country music industry any longer, as she was in Winchester. She would live right in the thick of it. Next, she went to work securing a manager. She found one in Randy Hughes. He had worked for Ferlin Husky and was married to Kathy Copas, country singer Lloyd "Cowboy" Copas' daughter. Hughes knew the music business and he believed in Patsy. More importantly he matched her determination.

In Patsy's last letter to Treva, we barely glimpse her future plans. Charlie is nearing the end of his army duty. Patsy mistakenly thinks her contract will end in May, but she was obligated to 4 Star for the entire year. She has plans for new recording sessions, but there's no talk of television or concert appearances. The year has yet to unfold, as does her career. And that is where we will leave her, with the future bright and unknown.

Jan 22/59
Winchester, Va

Dear Treva & all:

Just a few lines to say hello and hope your trip was a good one up and back. I've been trying to catch up on my letter writing and I don't remember if I've answered your last letter or not so I'll scribble a few lines now.

I sure did enjoy having you all stop in and I wish you could drop in now and hear my new recordings I a demo on each of them. I really have some thing different this time. The one I recorded with harmony with myself sounds great, If I do say so because every one is just flipping over it. It's called "Yes I Understand" and will be my next release I hope.

Owen Bradley (A+R for Decca) says he wants to give me 6% on new contract and terms any way I want them so

I guess I might as well stay with Decca after May. He wants to record a standard album + sacred album, as soon as 4 Star is up. The standard album will include songs like "Love Sick Blues", "St. Louis Blues", "Waltz of the Angels", "Oh Lonesome Time", "A Good Man Is Hard To Find", "Tra-le-le Dee Dee", "Beaten Heart" and then maybe a few new ones to wind it up. Anyway I'm real glad that I can do songs like those to be on records because I like them real good.

How is everything like snow + rain where you are? We have 6 in. of snow here. Fell last Fri + Sat. and it's pouring down here yesterday + tonite and more snow to come they say. I sure hope not. Charlie only has about 3 or 4 more weeks to go yet and then I'll be the happyest girl I know of. Ha.

Julie is fine and we took color pictures last sun. If good I'll send you one. Tell all hello + write soon. Love — Patsy + Julie"

P.S. Treva, I don't mind, our doing for Bonnie Lou and give her my best wishes for good luck and when Charles & I move to Nashville around April 1st or last we can get the fan club started again & the money because I'll be a regular on Opry & Hubert Long & Randy Hughes will manage & book me then. Hubert's Ferlin & Faron's manager & Randy works for Hubert & does Faron's bookings.

I wrote my first song today called "A Sometime Marriage." I'll send you the words later on.

Jan. 22/59
Winchester, Va.

Dear Treva and All:

Just a few lines to say "hello" and hope your trip was a good one up and back. I've been trying to catch up on my letter writing and I don't remember if I've answered your last letter or not so I'll scribble a few lines now.

I sure did enjoy having you all stop in and I wish you could drop in now and hear my new recordings. I've a demo on each of them. I really have something different this time.

The one I recorded with harmony with myself sounds great, if I do say so because everyone is just flipping over it. It's called "Yes I Understand," and will be my next release I hope.

Owen Bradley (A&R for Decca) says he wants to give me 6% on new contract and terms any way I want them so I guess I might as well stay with Decca after May. He wants to record a standard album and sacred album, as soon as 4 Star is up. The standard album will include songs like "Love Sick Blues," "St. Louis Blues," "Waltz of The Angels," "Oh Lonesome Time," "A Good Man Is Hard To Find," "Tweeddle Dee Dee," "Cheatin' Heart," and then maybe a few new ones to wind it up. Any way I'm real glad that I can do songs like those to be on records because I like them real good.

How is everything like snow and rain where you are? We have 6 in. of snow here. Fell last Fri and Sat. and it's pouring down here yesterday and tonite and more snow to come they say. I sure hope not. Charlie only has about 3 or 4 more weeks to go yet and then I'll be the happiest girl I know of. Ha.

Julie is fine and we took color pictures last Sun. If good I'll send you one. Tell all "hello" and write soon. Love Patsy and Julie.

P.S. Treva, I don't mind your doing for Bonnie Lou and give my best wishes for good luck and when Charles and I to Nashville around April

1st or last we can get the fan club started again and the money because I'll be a regular on Opry and Herbert Long and Randy Hughes will manage book me then. Herbert's Ferlin's and Faron's manager and Randy works for Herbert and does Faron's bookings.

I wrote my first song today called "A Sometime Marriage." I'll send you the words later on.

Patsy never recorded the song she wrote titled "A Sometime Marriage."

Patsy backstage a "Town and Country Jamboree."
From Treva's personal scrapbook, courtesy of Bruce Steinbicker.

Patsy, Treva and Bruce wearing hillbilly hats at Hillbilly Homecoming.
From Treva's scrapbook, courtesy Bruce Steinbicker.

Epilogue

We don't know why this collection of letters ends in January 1959, but we suspect that the correspondence continued long after that. Treva and Bruce were living with her mother and aunt, and the whole family moved to another house down the road about a mile away. Although their address remained the same, Rt. 1 in Telford, that move marks the end of this collection of correspondence. Our guess is that Treva packed away Patsy's letters when she moved, and as she received new letters she put them in a different place.

Patsy and Treva's friendship remained strong. In August 1959, Treva and Bruce stopped in at Winchester on their annual drive to Pennsylvania. Patsy, Charlie, and Julie were living in a nice little suburban ranch house, and the two families had an enjoyable visit. Treva and Bruce stayed about an hour and a half.

On September 17, 1960, Bruce was driving Treva and her family to Knoxville to visit relatives. They'd barely left town when their car was struck by a drunk driver. Treva was killed instantly. Her mother and aunt were badly hurt. Bruce's leg was injured. Emotionally he was devastated. The other driver got out of his car and ran from the scene. The police caught him within a few days.

One month later, Bruce entered the army, where he served as a disc jockey for Armed Services Radio in San Juan, Puerto Rico. A young woman named Ruthie Collins began writing to him. Her sister had been a member of the Louvin Brothers Fan Club, the same club through which Bruce had met Treva, and Ruthie had learned of Treva's death. She wrote to offer her condolences and Bruce responded to her letter. One letter followed another and eventually they met while he was on leave. They married in February 1962. Happily married, they have one son, Bruce David, Jr., and two grandchildren, Natalie and Seth.

In civilian life Bruce gave up his disc jockey aspirations and became an accountant. Still, he never lost his enthusiasm for the traditional country music he loved as a youth. He reflects on the changes in the music from its homespun origins to the commercial powerhouse that it is today. Is there still grassroots support for artists like Treva gave to Patsy?

On June 14, 1961, less than nine months after Treva's haunting death, Patsy was involved in a head-on crash with another vehicle. One person, a young mother, was killed. Four others, including the woman's five-year-old son, were badly hurt. Patsy was thrown through the windshield. Besides suffering scarring facial cuts, she broke her wrist and dislocated her hip. Her injuries landed her in the hospital for a month, no doubt giving her too much time to think about her close brush with the same fate that took her young friend.

Though Patsy had been slowed down, her career was gaining momentum. "I Fall to Pieces" was climbing the charts. On July 22, Patsy appeared on the Opry stage in a wheelchair. In mid-August she recorded her next big hit, "Crazy," a song that Willie Nelson had penned.

In his book "It's a Long Story: My Life," Willie wrote that after Patsy's husband, Charlie, heard Willie play the demo, he insisted they drive to the house to play the song for Patsy. Even though it was 1 A.M. and he'd have to wake his wife. Patsy liked the song and recorded it in mid-August, still on crutches. The Jordanaires, who backed Elvis Presley and many other singers, added harmonies.

Patsy's songs "I Fall to Pieces," "Crazy," and "She's Got You" became hits. Her days of obscurity and poverty were over. The Nashville

Sound, the recording style Owen helped create for her, changed the direction of the music away from its rural, "hillbilly" origin. Many of her recordings crossed over to the pop charts, which is rare for a country artist even now but especially at that time. Yet Patsy never lost her love for traditional country songs and she frequently performed them on her live shows .

While Patsy was writing to Treva, she longed for more time at home. In interviews she said that she planned to reduce her touring schedule. That never happened. On March 5, 1963, returning from a show in Kansas City, Patsy lost her life along with Cowboy Copas, Hawkshaw Hawkins, and her manager, Randy Hughes, when their plane went down. Julie was four years old. Her son, Randy, was two.

Charlie eventually remarried and had another son, Chip. That marriage ended in divorce. Until his death he was fiercely loyal to Patsy's memory and to his children. Julie is married and has three children (a fourth child was killed in an automobile accident). She is active in keeping Patsy's memory alive. Randy prefers to stay out of the limelight. Patsy's mother, Hilda Hensley, died in 1998 at the age of eighty-two. Patsy would be proud of her legacy, of her children, and of her music.

The marker that Charlie had placed on Patsy's grave reads in part, "Death cannot kill what never dies." Those words ring true whenever we hear one of Patsy's songs today. She sounds as fresh as she did in the studio nearly forty years ago. Patsy lived the songs she performed and so gave them that emotion we feel today. She has transcended all labels that we place upon music. Among all the artists who have recorded for us, Patsy Cline stands unique, timeless, and immortal.

Timeline

July 1955 Patsy records in her first session four songs: "Hiding Out," "Turn the Cards Slowly," "A Church, a Courtroom, and Then Goodbye," "Honky Tonk Merry Go Round." The session takes place in Nashville.

July 1, 1955 Patsy debuts on the Grand Old Opry singing "A Church, a Courtroom, and Then Goodbye." She is introduced by Ernest Tubb.

July 20,1955 Coral Records (a subsidiary of Decca) releases "A Church, a Courtroom, and Then Goodbye" and "Honky Tonk Merry Go Round" as Patsy's first single.

November 5, 1955 Coral releases Patsy's second single, "Hiding Out" and "Turn the Cards Slowly."

December 1955 Patsy becomes a cast member on the television show on WMAL Washington, D.C. The show is broadcast live on Saturday nights from ten to one.

December 18, 1955 Patsy records in Nashville, but no information on the session is now known.

January 5, 1956 Patsy records "Come On In," "I Love You Honey," "I Cried All the Way to the Altar," and "I Don't Wanta" in Nashville, according to accepted discography.

February 5, 1956 Coral releases "Come On In" and "I Love You Honey."

March 18, 1956 *The Washington Star* newspaper publishes an article on Patsy Cline and the "Town and Country Jamboree" television show.

April 13, 1956 Patsy and Charlie Dick meet for the first time.

April 22, 1956 Patsy records "Stop, Look, and Listen," "I've Loved and Lost Again," "Dear God," and "He Will Do for You" in Nashville.

April 27, 1956 Patsy rides in the Apple Blossom Festival parade. Her car banner reads, "Town and Country TV Star Patsy Cline."

June 16, 1956 Patsy sings "A Church, a Courtroom, and Then Goodbye" and "I've Loved and Lost Again" on the Grand Ole Opry.

July 8, 1956 Decca releases "Stop, Look, and Listen" and "I've Loved and Lost Again." Patsy is no longer on Coral, Decca's subsidiary label.

November 8, 1956 Patsy records "Walkin' After Midnight," "The Heart You Break May Be Your Own," "Pick Me Up on Your Way Down," and "A Poor Man's Roses" in Nashville.

December 1956 Patsy discovers that Arthur Godfrey wants her to perform on his television show, *Arthur Godfrey's Talent Scouts*.

January 21, 1957 Patsy performs "Walkin' After Midnight" on the Godfrey show, to a national audience. She wins first place in the talent contest.

February 1957 Patsy quit *the* "Town and Country" show.

February 11, 1957 Decca releases "Walkin' After Midnight" and "A Poor Man's Roses."

February 16, 1957 Patsy sings "Walkin' After Midnight" on the Grand Ole Opry.

March 14, 1957 Patsy performs on the *Town Hall Party*, a country music show syndicated on television as the *Western Ranch Party*, and on *The Bob Crosby Show*, a popular variety show in Hollywood.

March 28, 1957 Patsy and Gerald Cline obtain their divorce.

April 24, 1957 Patsy records "Today, Tomorrow, and Forever," "Fingerprints," "A Stranger in My Arms," and "Don't Ever Leave Me

Again." She also per forms on the *Arthur Godfrey and His Friends* show.

April 25, 1957 Patsy records "Try Again," "Too Many Secrets," "Then You'll Know," and "Three Cigarettes in an Ashtray," all in New York.

May 1957 Patsy rides in the Apple Blossom Festival parade in Winchester again.

May 23, 1957 Patsy records "That Wonderful Someone," "In Care of the Blues," "Hungry for Love," "I Can't Forget," "I Don't Wanta," and "Ain't No Ships on This Wheel."

May 27, 1957 Decca releases "Today, Tomorrow, and Forever" and " Try Again."

July 26, 1957 Patsy appears on Alan Freed's rock and roll show, *Big Beat.*

August 5, 1957 Decca releases the LP *Patsy Cline*, her first long-play album, and two extended-play (four songs) albums, *Patsy Cline* and, on Coral, *Songs by Patsy Cline.*

August 12, 1957 Decca releases "Three Cigarettes in an Ashtray" and "A Stranger in My Arms."

September 1957 The magazine *Folk and Country Songs* lists Patsy as one of the top ten country singers.

September 15, 19 57 Patsy and Charlie marry at her mother's home in Winchester.

October 25, 1957 Patsy performs on Arthur Godfrey's show again.

November 15-16, 1957 Patsy receives awards at the annual Disc Jockey convention in Nashville for "Walkin' After Midnight." *Billboard* gives her an award for Most Promising Country and Western Female Artist, and *Music Vendor* gives her one for Greatest Achievement in Records.

November 18, 1957 Decca releases "I Don 't Wanta " and "Then You'll Know."

December 13, 1957 Patsy records "Stop the World," "Walking

Dream," "Cry Not for Me," and "If I Could See the World" in Nashville.

January 13, 1958 Decca releases "Stop the World" and "Walking Dream."

February 14, 1958 Patsy finishes her only recording session of 1958, recording six songs: " Come On In," "Let the Teardrops Fall," "I Can See an Angel," "Never No More," "If I Could See the World," and "Just Out of Reach."

June 2, 1958 Decca releases "Come On In" and "Let the Teardrops Fall."

June 20, 1958 Treva and Bruce marry.

August 18, 1958 Decca releases "I Can See an Angel" and "Never No More."

August 25, 1958 Julie Dick is born.

September 9, 1958 Decca releases "If I Could See the World" and "Just Out of Reach."

December 15, 1958 Decca releases "Dear God" and "He Will Do for You."

January 8, 1959 Patsy records "I'm Moving Along," 'I'm Blue Again," and "Love, Love, Love Me Honey Do."

January 9, 1959 Patsy records " Yes, I Understand" and "Gotta Lot of Rhythm in My Soul" in Nashville. She is recorded in stereo for the first time, and the Jordanaires sing backup for the first time.

February 1959 Charlie receives his honorable discharge from the army.

February 23, 1959 Decca releases "Yes, I Understand" and "Cry Not for Me." August or September 1959 Patsy, Charlie, and Julie move to Nashville.

September 17, 1960 Treva is killed in an auto accident.

PATSY CLINE

www.ingramcontent.com/pod-product-compliance
Lightning Source LLC
Chambersburg PA
CBHW020438130626
46549CB00001B/200